Troubleshooting and Repairing Power Tools

Troubleshooting and Repairing Power Tools

Homer L. Davidson

TAB BOOKS

Blue Ridge Summit, PA

FIRST EDITION
SECOND PRINTING

© 1990 by **TAB Books**.
TAB Books is a division of McGraw-Hill, Inc.

Printed in the United States of America. All rights reserved. The publisher takes no
responsibility for the use of any of the materials or methods described in this book,
nor for the products thereof.

Library of Congress Cataloging-in-Publication Data

Davidson, Homer L.
    Troubleshooting and repairing power tools / by Homer L. Davidson.
        p.   cm.
    Includes index.
    ISBN 0-8306-7347-4   ISBN 0-8306-3347-2 (pbk.)
    1. Power tools—Maintenance and repair.   I. Title.
TT153.5.D38   1990
621.9—dc20   90-37846
                                                              CIP

TAB Books offers software for sale. For information and a catalog, please contact
TAB Software Department, Blue Ridge Summit, PA 17294-0850.

Questions regarding the content of this book should be addressed to:

Reader Inquiry Branch
TAB Books
Blue Ridge Summit, PA 17294-0850

Acquisitions Editor: Kimberly Tabor
Book Editor: Cherie R. Blazer
Production: Katherine G. Brown
Book Design: Jaclyn J. Boone
Cover Photography: Brent Blair, Harrisburg, PA

Contents

Acknowledgments

*T*he many photos throughout the book cover power tools with various brand names: AMT, Black & Decker, Bostic, Bridgewood, Craftsman, Dremel, Makita, Menards, Ram, Roybi, Rockwell, Sears, Skil, Swingline, Weed Eater, Weller and Williams & Hussey.

To the manufacturers who furnished photos and permission to use valuable service data, I owe a great deal of thanks: American Machine and Tool Company, Campbell-Hausfeld Co., Delta Machinery Corp., Foley-Belsaw Co., Freud USA Inc., and Wilke Machinery Co.

The "old timer" to whom I refer in the text could easily be my father, who was a carpenter and builder in the trades.

Introduction

*P*ower tools may last a lifetime if properly maintained, lubricated, and repaired. They come in several shapes and sizes, from large floor models to bench and portable tools. For years those power tools were operated from the power line; now you can operate many different cordless power tools from self-contained rechargeable batteries.

Cordless power tools range in size from the small screwdriver to the circular power saw. These cordless tools operate from nickel-cadmium batteries, which may be recharged in 1 or 3 hours. The heavy-duty circular cordless power saw can cut up to 125 2 × 4s with one charge. The benefit of these cordless tools is that they can do work where power lines and extension cords are not available.

The power tool is run by a motor at high speeds. Large power tools might operate with a $1^1/_2$ or $2^1/_2$ horsepower motor, while a cordless screwdriver will have only a fractional horsepower motor. Some direct current (dc) motors found in the cordless power tools have reverse and forward operations.

The woodworking tool is only as good as the person who uses it. In addition to knowing how to operate each tool, you must know the safety factor with each power tool. Remember, these power tools can be dangerous. You can quickly lose a finger or hand, or cut yourself badly before you know how it happened. Learn the safety rule of each power tool. Practice safety in your woodworking shop or room every minute. This is not to say that you should be afraid of power tools; just know how to operate them safely.

Making things with your own hands provides a great deal of satisfaction and pride and can be just plain fun. Knowing how to keep your power tools in top shape and how to repair them when they break down will save valuable time and money. Anyone who operates power tools can learn how to repair them by simply reading this book.

We will start out by learning power tool basics in Chapter 1. Correct operation and safety are very important. Keep tools grounded for safe working conditions. Know what to do when the power tool begins to smoke or slow down. You can quickly check the continuity of that power tool with the digital multimeter.

Proper care of power tools, from cleanup to lubrication and inspection provides longer power tool operations. Chapter 2 provides tips on tool care and operation. Also listed are the various tools needed to service most power tools, many of which you will find in your shop.

In Chapter 3 you will be able to find out what type of motor operates the various power tools in your shop, how they work, and how to check them. A motor troubleshooting chart is found at the end of the chapter.

Chapter 4 lists all the simple repairs you can do yourself, with Chapter 5 providing instructions on how to clean up and lubricate the power tools. Included are tips on when and when not to use grease and oil, and how to clean up and maintain tools and metal tables.

Nickel-cadmium batteries are the topic of Chapter 6. Because they are the power source for cordless tools, you will need to know how to service, change, and charge these batteries. Also included are steps to repair six different small cordless power tools.

Chapter 7 provides photo and data on how to maintain small power tools, Chapter 8 covers medium power tools, Chapter 9 focuses on large power tools.

Learn how to purchase, clean up, and repair power tools picked up at garage sales and flea markets in Chapter 10. You will also find a glossary and a list of manufacturers' addresses. Now, let's get started.

Chapter **1**

Power tool basics

Building and constructing wood or metal projects with power tools can be a source of pride and self satisfaction, and is just plain fun. Remember: the tools are only as good as the person who knows how to use them. Keeping those tools in top shape and being able to troubleshoot and repair them can save you time and money, and will make your work more enjoyable (FIG. 1-1).

1-1 Keep power tools in top shape by troubleshooting and repairing them yourself.

SAFETY RULES

Almost anyone can learn how to use power tools, but using them correctly and safely is another story. It's simple: Read the manufacturer's operating instructions that come with the owner's manual. Power tools can be dangerous, so be wide awake and careful at all times.

When using electric power tools, keep the following basic safety rules in mind to help prevent personal injury, electrical shock, and risk of fire. Specific tools will have specific safety rules; follow these as well.

- Read the operating manual before using the power tool.
- Keep safety guards and covers in place. Do not remove them and forget to put them back.
- Wear safety glasses, even if you now wear a pair of glasses (FIG. 1-2). Use a dust mask when cutting or during dusty operations.

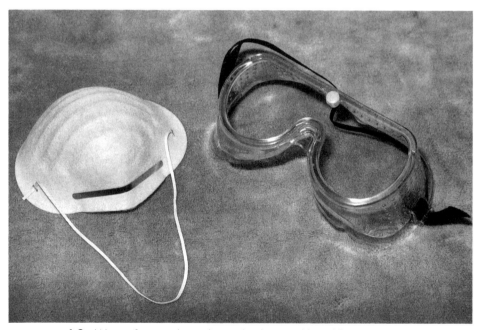

1-2 Wear safety goggles and a mask when working with power tools.

- Keep benches and work area clean. Clean up after every job to prevent accidents.
- Never use ac power tools in the rain or in any damp or wet locations. Work on a rubber mat to prevent possible shock.
- Do not use tools around paint or flammable liquids.

- Keep work area well lighted.
- Keep children away from power tools. Never talk to visitors while tools are operating. Operate your own tools.
- Turn off all electricity with one large fuse box switch. Padlock shop door and starting switches.
- Store idle tools in racks or cabinets, away from children.
- Don't force the power tool; use it only for the job it was designed to do. Do not force a small power tool to do the job of a heavyweight.
- Disconnect tools before servicing or changing bits, blades, or cutters. Remove the key before starting any power tool.
- Make sure the switch is off before plugging in the power tool.
- Don't overreach: Keep yourself balanced with both feet on the floor. Turn off the power tool before reaching for something a few feet away.
- Do not wear loose clothing, large sleeves, jewelry, neckties or other things that could get caught in moving parts.
- Remove all keys and wrenches before turning on the power tool. Keep these tools in a proper place.
- Keep all tools sharp and clean for better performance and to prevent damage. Follow the manufacturer's instructions.
- Do not abuse the power cord. Never carry the tool by the cord. Do not give the cord a yank to remove from the power source. Keep the cord from being cut by the tool, and away from heat, oil, and wet conditions. Repair all frayed cords.
- Use clamps or a vise to hold work when using power tools. This prevents damage to hands and keeps both hands free to operate the power tool.
- When using extension cords, select the correct type for outdoors. Never use an underrated or cheap power cord on heavy-duty power tools. Do not use any extension cord outdoors in the rain.
- Check power tools for damaged parts. These should be replaced and repaired before operating. Check for proper alignment, binding, breakage, mounting, and any other conditions that could affect the operation of the power tool.
- Don't walk or stand on power tools.
- Never leave the power tool running or operating to answer the phone, while talking to someone or for any other reason. Shut it off and make sure the power tool has stopped.
- Feed the work into the blade or cutter against the direction of rotation. Make sure the material is flat and solid while feeding it into the blade or cutter.

- Make sure all power tools are grounded to prevent electrical shock. Do not work around pipes, radiators, or grounded surfaces without properly grounding the power tool.
- When servicing the power tool, always use the manufacturer's identical replacement part.
- Do not use accessories that are not recommended by the manufacturer.
- Do not operate the power tool if you are tired. Watch what you are doing at all times; be alert. Do not go to the workshop after a very tiresome or upsetting day.

GROUNDING POWER TOOLS

All power tools fastened to the workbench should be grounded at the receptacle power box and metal base plate. Use at least Number 10 or 12 copper wire. Portable power tools are grounded with a three-prong plug. Do not cut off the grounding pin to fit in an ungrounded receptacle or extension cord. If the power outlet does not have a three-prong outlet, use a grounding adaptor (FIG. 1-3).

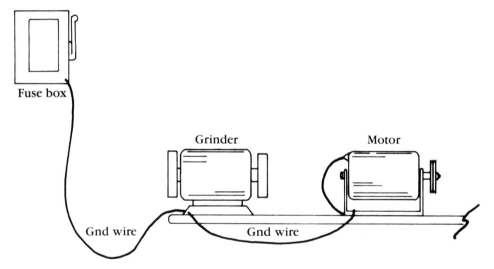

Fuse box

Grinder   Motor

Gnd wire   Gnd wire

1-3 Ground all power tools. Use the power line ground, and connect large power tools together with Number 10 or 12 copper wire.

Improper grounding heightens the risk of electrical shock. Usually, the grounded wire conductor is green with or without yellow stripes. If in doubt, when changing a defective power cord or plug, use the ohmmeter or digital multimeter to check the continuity between the ground wire (green) and the power tool (FIG. 1-4).

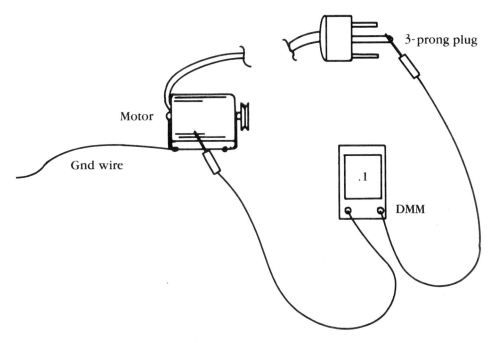

1-4 Use the ohmmeter or digital multimeter to check for good ground between green wire of the three-prong polarized plug and the power tool.

If your shop does not have grounded power outlets, install them or call a qualified electrician. Check the grounded receptacle; do not take chances. The time it takes could save your life! The common ground from the fuse box should be attached to the ground terminal of the ac receptacle. Use only three-wire extension cords that have three-prong grounding plugs with three-pole receptacles.

Check for proper ground at the outlet or power tool with the digital multimeter. Measure the ac voltage at the receptacle between the hot terminal and the ground terminal or metal box (FIG. 1-5). Try both terminals, one at a time, to the ground terminal. If there is low or no ac voltage measurement, improper grounding is a probable cause.

FUSE PROTECTION

All ac power tools should be protected with the correct fuse. Make sure the workbenches and each large power tool are protected with a fuse box that can be turned off when trouble arises (FIG. 1-6). Ac power tools up to 1½ horsepower can be operated from 15- and 20-amp fuse boxes. Fuse both sides of the line when operating 220-volt power tools. Large power tools with 2½ horsepower or larger motors may be fused with 30-amp cartridge fuses. If in doubt, check with your local electrician. All fuses can be checked with the low range of the ohmmeter.

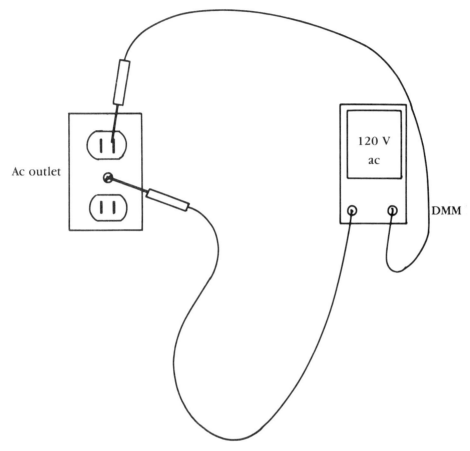

1-5   Check out the ground of the polarized ac plug with a digital multimeter set at 200 volts ac.

EXTENSION CORD SAFETY

If you must use an extension cord, use only the three-wire cords that have three-prong grounding type plugs and sockets. All extension cords should be repaired or replaced if cut, worn, or damaged. A rough estimate of extension cord length with power tool amperage should be Number 16 wire for 15 feet or less, Number 14 wire for 50 feet or less, and Number 12 wire for 100 feet or less. Of course, this will depend upon the amperage of the power tool (TABLE 1-1).

All extension cords should be recommended by the Underwriters Laboratories (UL) rating. If the extension cord is used outside, the cord must be suitable for indoor use. "WA" on the cord jacket indicates that the cord can be used outdoors. Usually, any cord marked for outdoor use can be used indoors.

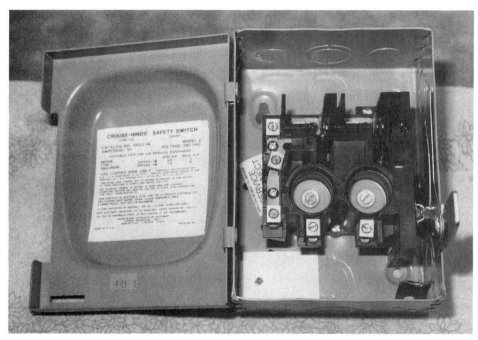

1-6 Use a fuse box to protect each large power tool and one box for the workbench. Fuse both sides of the power line.

Table 1-1. Correct Wire Gauge Usage

Name Plate	Cord Length in Feet					
Amps	25	50	100	150	175	200
0-3	18 ga.	18 ga.	18 ga.	16 ga.	14 ga.	12 ga.
3-6	18	18	16	14	12	12
6-8	18	16	14	12	12	12
8-10	18	16	14	12	12	12
10-13	16	16	14	12	12	12
13-15	14	14	12	12	12	12

Remember, the smaller the wire gauge number, the greater the carrying capacity of the extension cord. For instance, the 12-gauge wire is larger and carries a higher amperage power tool than the 18-gauge wire. It's best to use one long extension cord rather than two or three different power cords to cover an area. Never use extension cords in the rain or in other wet or damp locations.

SMOKING TOOLS

Always shut the power off when the power tool begins to smoke. Often, the motor is overheated and overworked. The bearings might be dry and could freeze up. If the armature is prevented from rotating, the field coils get red hot. Keep the motor air holes open. Clean out all dust and dirt (FIG. 1-7). Lubricate the motor, if necessary. Smoke can be a sign of dull bits and saw blades. Sharpen the saw blades when the wood begins to show burned spots.

I-7 Clean out sawdust and dirt from the vent holes of large motors if they become overheated and begin to smoke.

SHARPENING TOOLS

A dull saw blade can result in burned marks on the material, slow feeding, and rough cut edges. The dull drill bit might stop removing material, plus it could jam and cause damage to the drill.

Have dull saw blades sharpened by a professional, unless you have the tools to do so. Practically anyone can sharpen drill bits. Compare the dull drill bit with a correctly sharpened bit to determine the heel to point cut (FIG. 1-8). The heel is about 10 to 12 degrees lower than the edge of the lip. The flute area may be grounded out by placing it over the corner of the wheel (FIG. 1-9). You can also purchase a drill bit sharpener. Just drop the bit in the sharpener and turn on the power.

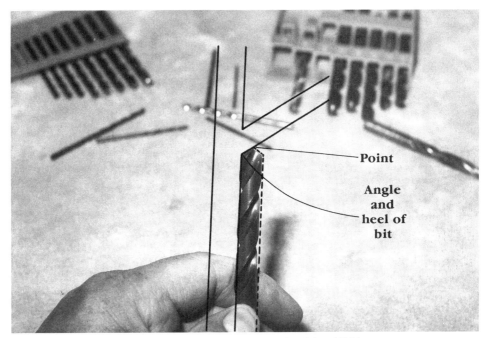

I-8 Check the heel to point angle of the drill bit.

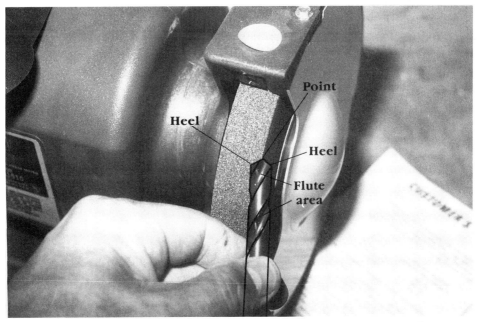

I-9 To remove some of the flute area of the bit, place it over the corner of the grinding wheel.

MOTOR BELT PROBLEMS

A defective motor belt might be cracked, slick, or worn extensively on both sides. The slick belt can be repaired with belt dressing. The old method called for an application of beeswax on the motor belt, which created better traction. Sometimes the belt will become stiff with age or lack of use. Replace the defective belt with one the exact size and type.

Check for proper alignment of motor and pulleys when the belt begins to wear on one side. A horizontal belt drive is better than a vertical drive for good traction and tension (FIG. 1-10). The center of the motor pulley must be in line with the center of the arbor or saw pulley. The motor base mount should be adjustable so it can be lined up in either direction with both pulleys.

1-10   The horizontal belt drive works better than a vertical drive. The belt is kept tight with the flexible base plate.

SANDING BELT PROBLEMS

Make sure a new belt is lined up properly. The underside arrow should rotate in the direction of the moving belt, and the belt should travel against the work stop plate. Abrasive belts are designed to operate in one direction only. Most power tools have a tension adjustment to center the belt. With a new belt, adjust the alignment for correct tracking, readjusting until the belt is running in line.

Three different abrasives are used on sanding belts: aluminum oxide, silicon carbide, and garnet. Although higher in price, aluminum oxide and silicon carbide are best for general sanding, and for hardwoods and metals. Garnet abrasive works best on softwoods and composition board (TABLE 1-2).

Table 1-2. Usage of Abrasives

Abrasive	*Use*	*Rough*	*Medium*	*Fine*
Aluminum Oxide	Hardboard	11/2−21/2	1/2−1/0	2/0−3/0
	Copper	40−50	80−100	100−200
	Steel	24−30	60−80	100
	Plastic	50−80	120−180	240
Silicon Carbide	Glass	50−60	100−120	12−320
	Cast Iron	24−30	60−80	100
Garnet	Hardboard	11/2−21/2	1/2−1/0	2/0−3/0
	Softwood	11/2−1	1/0	2/0
	Composition Board	11/2−1	1/2	1/0
	Plastic	11/2	1/2−1/0	2/0−3/0

MARKING TOOLS

Mark each power tool with an engraver. This can prevent theft and help you identify your tools (FIG. 1-11). Use your social security number or something similar as the identifier, then record each power tool in a notebook with dates purchased and serial numbers. Take several photos of all the power tools in the room. The camcorder is handy to identify tools in the unfortunate event of a fire or break-in. It is difficult to remember how many different tools you have acquired when the insurance adjuster comes around.

ASSEMBLING TOOLS

Most medium-sized or larger power tools are packaged with some disassembled parts. You must be able to put all the components together. First read the instruction manual, which often includes step-by-step assembly procedures.

Make sure all components are tight and in line before firing up the power tool. Rotate the wheel or pulleys by hand to make sure nothing is rubbing or binding. Retighten all mounting and assembly screws.

DISASSEMBLING TOOLS

Visually inspect the entire power tool before tearing it down for repairs. Place all screws and bolts in cups or containers so they will not be misplaced or lost. Draw an outline of all parts or lay them in line as they are taken apart (FIG. 1-12). Remove only the parts that are needed to get at the defective component. Reverse the procedure to assemble the parts of the power tool after replacing defective parts.

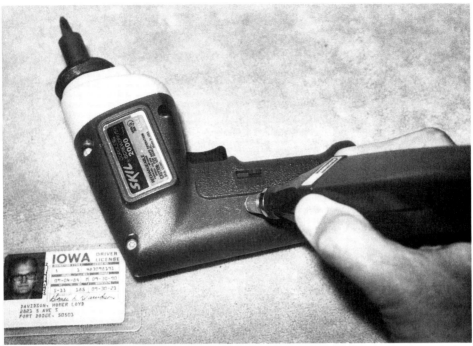

1-11 Use an engraver to mark each power tool for identification and in case of fire or theft.

1-12 Draw an outline and mark down the placement of each part, or lay them out in a line so they can be easily replaced.

CHECKING TOOLS WITH A VOM OR DMM

The voltohmmeter (VOM) or digital multimeter (DMM) can help locate defective components (FIG. 1-13). Select a DMM if you have to buy a test instrument. Choose a DMM with an audible readout for making continuity measurements. Not only can you see the resistance measurement, you can hear it.

1-13 Use an ohmmeter or digital multimeter to check continuity, voltage, and resistance of various parts of the tool, and to identify the defective ones. New digital multimeters have audible readout; intermittent connections produce a crackling sound.

Use the low-resistance ohmmeter scale to take continuity readings across the ac plug terminals. This will reveal if a coil winding, armature winding, cord, or ac switch are open—meaning voltage is not moving to these components. Check the continuity of the motor terminals to see if the dc motor is open or has dirty contacts or brushes (FIG. 1-14). Take dc voltage measurements at the motor terminals to determine if the battery or motor is defective (FIG. 1-15). Likewise, ac voltage measurement at the larger ac motor terminals may determine if voltage is reaching the motor terminals. The digital multimeter is ideal for checking defective switches, cords, and fuses.

USING THE SOLDERING GUN

The 200-watt soldering gun is ideal to solder up connections and terminals in power tools (FIG. 1-16). When using the soldering gun, first open it up for inspection by removing external screws (FIG. 1-17). Make sure the cord and plug are not defective by checking the cord continuity from plug to switch.

Check the on/off switch with the low ohm scale of the digital multimeter to make sure there are no defective switch contacts (FIG. 1-18). Replace any defective switches with exact replacements. Figure 1-19 is a diagram of a typical dual-heating soldering gun. Many problems that arise with this tool are from defective tips, switches, and cords.

A broken or cracked gun body may be repaired with epoxy cement and a coat of black auto enamel.

1-14   Check the resistance or continuity of the motor winding to see if it is open or has dirty brushes or contacts.

1-15   If the motor does not rotate, measure the voltage applied to it. Here 2.55 volts is applied to the dc motor terminals.

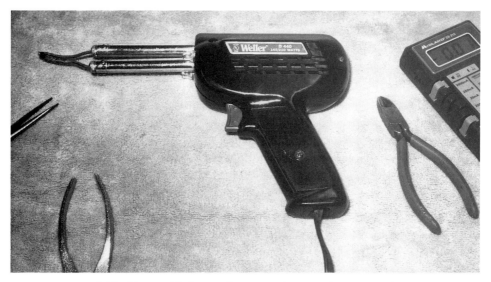

I-16 Use a soldering gun for connecting parts in power tools.

I-17 Remove external screws to open up the soldering gun for inspection.

1-18   Check the on/off switch with the low ohm scale of digital multimeter to check for open, burned, or dirty contacts.

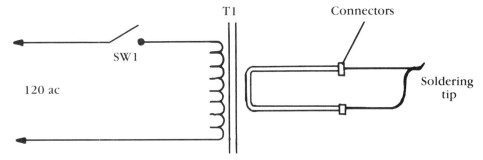

1-19   A typical schematic diagram of a dual-heat soldering gun. Most problems with the soldering gun are the result of defective tips, switches, and cords.

Chapter **2**

Proper care of power tools

Most power tools will last a lifetime if they are kept clean, treated well, and lubricated. Here are some tips: Power drills and electric saws work much better with sharp bits and saw blades. Correct use of the power tool will help prevent damaged gear box and bearings. Keep the batteries charged to help save battery replacement and keep the cordless power tool ready for action.

INSPECTING CORDS AND PLUGS

Check the power cord and plug each time you use it. When rubber power cords get old, the rubber cracks and peels off, which exposes wires. If the cord is damaged or cut in any way, replace it. Inspect the plug for frayed wires, cuts in the cord, or loose wires at the male plug (FIG. 2-1). These are very dangerous problems. Besides starting a fire, frayed or cut power cords may cause extensive shock or burns to the operator.

WALL OUTLETS

Plug power tools into three-prong outlets. The spade or third prong grounds the power tool metal body to a common ground (FIG. 2-2). Do not cut off the ground prong when it will not fit in the receptacle or extension cord, instead purchase a ground outlet receptacle (FIG. 2-3). The ground wire at the ac receptacle should be grounded to the main power switch block terminal. The bronze screw carries the hot or black wire, while the negative or white wire connects to the brass screw. The ground or green wire connects to the ground screw terminal.

SOLDERING CONNECTIONS

When repairing cords, components, or connections, solder with a soldering iron or gun. Otherwise, your tools may run erratically or intermittently. It is especially

17

important to solder the ac wires connected to the ac plug, as well as all switch and battery connections (FIG. 2-4). Make sure the ac cord connections inside the motor are soldered with twist type connectors. Use a 60/40 electronic solder for these connections (FIG. 2-5).

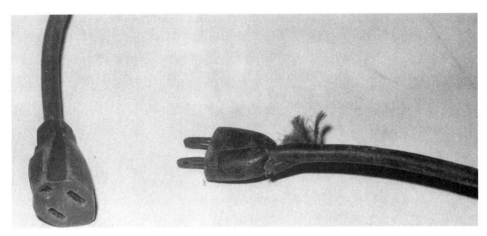

2-1   Inspect the power cord for cuts and frayed or loose wires.

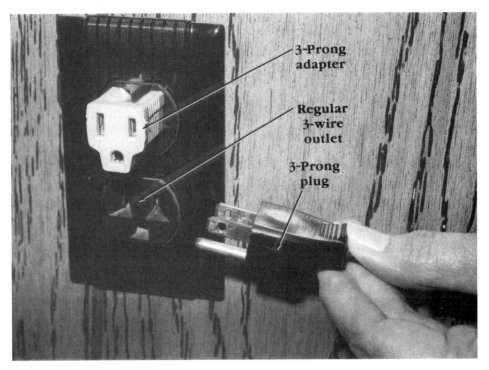

2-2   A typical grounded plug. Three prongs ground the power tool.

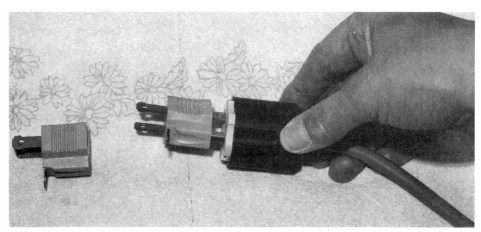

2-3 Do not cut off the ground terminal; use an adapter with a ground pin fastened to the metal outlet screw.

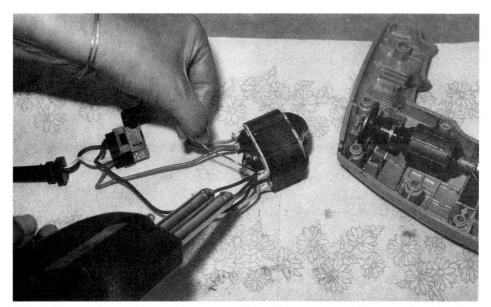

2-4 Solder up all connections to the power cable, switches, motor, and battery using the soldering iron.

KEEP BLADES SHARP

Keep saw blades sharp to prevent splintering, rough edges, and burn marks on the wood (FIG. 2-6). You can tell when the saw blade is getting dull if it requires a little more pressure to feed wood into the blade. Avoid buried nails or metal objects on the piece of wood that is being fed into the saw; these can quickly dull the blade.

2-5 Use 60/40 electronic solder.

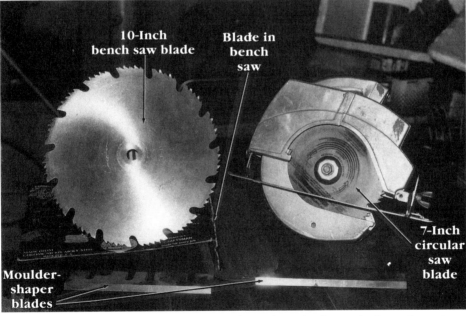

2-6 Keep the saw blades sharp to prevent burned, rough edges and splintered wood.

Leave the sharpening of circular saw blades up to a professional. Most hardware stores, carpenters, and repair shops can help you find someone who sharpens saw blades.

KEEP DRILL BITS SHARP

Sharpening drill bits (FIG. 2-7) is a much easier task than sharpening circular saw blades. Pick up a sharpening drill attachment if you want to sharpen your own bits. Do not use a lot of pressure on the drill bit when it slows up or begins to burn the wood; this is your sign that the bit needs sharpening.

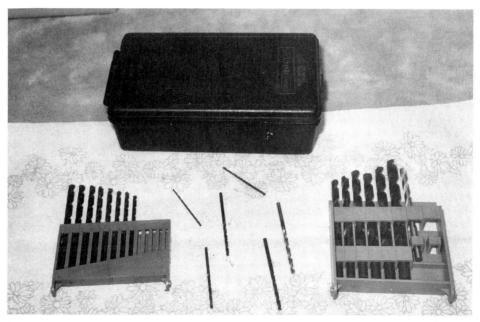

2-7 Keep drill bits sharp to prevent burning, smoking, and damage to the bit. Select the correct size bit for the type of work you are doing.

Always use the correct type of bit for the job, and use the bit correctly: For wood use twist bits, spade bits and power auger bits. For metal, use high-speed twist drill bits. For brick, cement, cinder block and masonry, use carbide-tipped bits. Before drilling, center punch at the point to be drilled. Do not stall motor by using too much pressure on the drill. Pull the drill out to clear the bit when drilling holes. Use cutting lubricant when drilling metal, except for cast iron and brass, which should be drilled dry. Aluminum may be drilled using kerosene as a lubricant. Remember, wood can be drilled with the same twist drills used for metal.

WARNING SOUNDS

Stop the power tool at once when unusual sounds such as screeching, thumping, whining and humming are heard. A dry bearing can produce a screeching sound, a defective belt the thumping or knocking noise, a defective motor the loud humming sound, a defective commutator the whining.

CORRECT WIRE SIZE

The power tool bench may be wired with Number 14 or 12 wire. Overall, Number 12 wire is the best and safest. The power bench should be fused with a double-pole double-throw (DPDT) circuit breaker. Larger stationary power tools should be wired with Number 8 or 10 electrical wire.

Choose a 15- or 20-amp fuse for the average power tool and have the main bench fuse turn off all power tools in the shop. Select the cartridge fuse circuit breaker box when high-powered tools are installed. Use Number 18 wire extension cords up to 50 feet and Number 16 up to 100 feet (TABLE 1-1). Check with the local electrician to ensure adequate and safe wiring.

BLOWN FUSES

Inspect the power tool if the fuse blows while you are using it. Check to see if the fuse is a 15- or 20-amp type. The fuse can blow when too many tools or appliances are operating upon one circuit. If the lights blink for a moment when a tool is started, this is normal. However, if the lights dim while the power bench saw or planer is operating, have an electrician install larger wire and place the power tools on another circuit. Insufficient line voltage at the power tool may cause extensive damage to the tool and the wiring, and could start a fire.

If the fuse still blows when replaced, perhaps you have a shorted power tool. Pull out all power tool cords, and screw a 25-watt bulb in place of the fuse. When the light bulb goes out, you have located the defective power tool (FIG. 2-8).

2-8   A light bulb screwed into the fuse socket might help locate the shorted power tool.

CLEANING AND RUST PREVENTION

Use a damp cloth with general household detergent to clean portable power tools. Do not use paint thinner, turpentine, or gasoline to clean off the plastic bodies because it might turn the plastic finish dull. Try to prevent liquids from getting inside the tool during cleaning.

Rub a light film of oil over the metal surfaces of power tools with a soft cloth to prevent rusting (FIG. 2-9). You can also use spray wax to prevent rust on metal tables. Spray the tabletop of a bench saw, planer, or drill with silicone oil spray. Keep these components free of dust and dirt. Clean the table with a stiff brush to prevent dust from clinging. Clean off cast iron parts with fine sandpaper or steel wool.

2-9   To prevent rust, use a cloth soaked with light oil to wipe off the metal parts on power tools..

ORDERING PARTS

Before attempting to obtain replacement parts, locate the part number. Look in the owner's manual for parts layout and a part number chart (FIG. 2-10). If the part number is not handy, take the model number of the tool and part to its place of purchase. Many manufacturers have service centers or depots for parts and repair. Check the owner's manual for service center listings. Check with the local appliance, electrical, and motor repairman for parts and repairs if the power tool is old.

DO'S AND DON'TS

- Don't use ac-powered tools in wet conditions.
- Don't break off the ground terminal of the 3-prong plug.
- Don't insert a penny or tin foil behind a blown fuse when you do not have another fuse on hand.
- Don't over oil power tools.

- Don't overwork or put extra pressure on a power tool to finish the job.
- Don't use a cracked grinder wheel; replace it at once.
- Do ground all ac power tools in the shop.
- Do repair all damaged plugs and cords.
- Do keep the shop and all tools as clean as possible.
- Do keep a light coat of oil upon metal power tool surfaces when not in use.
- Do check the power tool bearings and gear boxes when unusual noises are heard.
- Do keep batteries charged in the cordless power tools.
- Do keep safety guards over bench saws, shapers, and jointers.
- Do wear eye and dust protectors when operating power tools.
- Do use the correct wire size and grounded extension cord when working outside.
- Do keep power tool cords away from rotating teeth or drills.
- Do keep all saw blades, drills, and tools sharp.
- Do be wide awake at all times when operating power tools.
- Do install a main power switch to shut off all power tools and outlets in the shop.
- Do call a professional when you feel you need help repairing power tools. Take the power tool to the manufacturer's service center or a repair shop.

2-10 Look up the defective part in the parts list of the owner's manual. Take along the part and model numbers and the part itself when buying a replacement.

REQUIRED TOOLS FOR MAKING REPAIRS.

The basic items needed to repair shop tools can be found in practically every home: a flat screwdriver, pliers, long nose pliers, and soldering gun.

If you want to repair a wider range of power tools, add the following: a small flat screwdriver, a set of wrenches, a Phillips screwdriver, socket set, nut drivers, soldering iron, Allen wrenches, metal center punch, cold chisel, wire tool connector, side cutters, and tape.

A digital multimeter is also necessary for taking continuity, resistance, voltage, and diode tests (FIG. 2-11). Another handy gadget is a line neon voltage tester or a pigtail light bulb tester. The pigtail light bulb tester is made up of a 25- or 40-watt light bulb, pigtail socket, and alligator clips (FIG. 2-12). Pick one up at the electrical or hardware store.

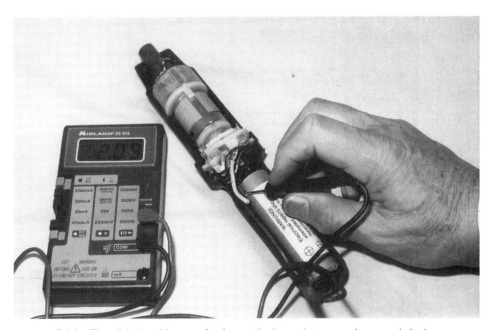

2-11 The digital multimeter checks continuity, resistance, voltage, and diodes.

TESTING SWITCHES

The on/off and speed switches are often the cause of erratic and intermittent tool operation, or the reason the tool stops running completely. Simply connect the ohmmeter across the switch terminals (FIG. 2-13). It should indicate a dead short. If so, clean up switch contacts with cleaning fluid. If resistance is above 1 ohm, replace the switch. Place the alligator clip lead across the switch terminals and if motor operates, install another switch.

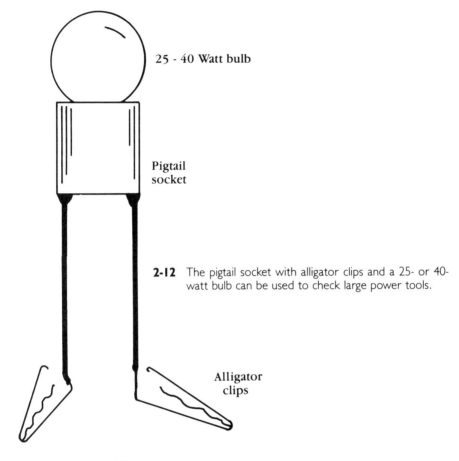

25 - 40 Watt bulb

Pigtail
socket

2-12   The pigtail socket with alligator clips and a 25- or 40-
watt bulb can be used to check large power tools.

Alligator
clips

CHECKING DIODES

Silicon diodes are easily tested with the diode test on the digital multimeter. Clip
the positive (red) probe to the negative (anode) terminal and negative (black)
probe to the cathode (+) terminal of the diode for a normal test (FIG. 2-14). The
open diode will have no measurement in any direction (FIG. 2-15). A shorted diode
will produce a low ohmmeter measurement with reversed test leads (FIG. 2-16).
Tests using the ohmmeter are the same, except for the resistance measurements.

CHECKING CAPACITORS

The small bypass capacitors across switch terminals or electrolytic capacitors in
split-phase motors may be checked with the small capacitor tester (FIG. 2-17). To
check if a small capacitor is charged, pull the motor plug and pass a screwdriver
blade across the capacitor terminals. If they spark, the capacitor is charged.
Always discharge large motor capacitors; if not, they can produce dangerous
shocks.

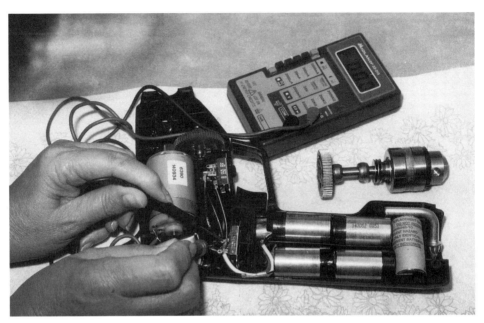

2-13 Check the switches with the ohmmeter. A defective switch can be open or have a reading above 2 ohms. Erratic measurement indicates a dirty or burned switch.

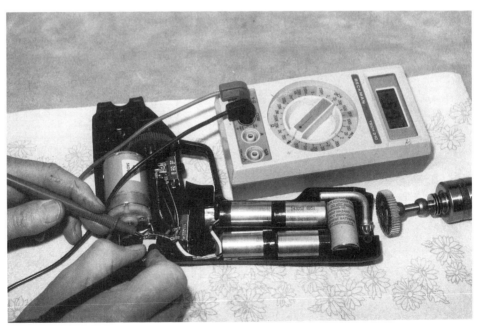

2-14 Checking the silicon diode for open, shorted, and normal tests.

2-15   The open diode will not measure in any direction.

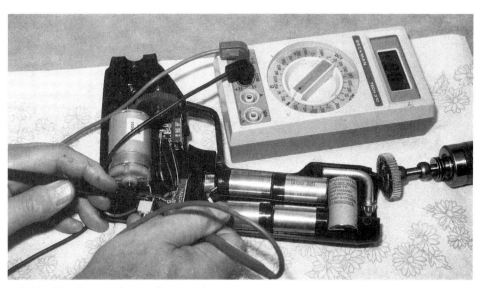

2-16   The shorted diode will show a low resistance measurement with reversed test leads.

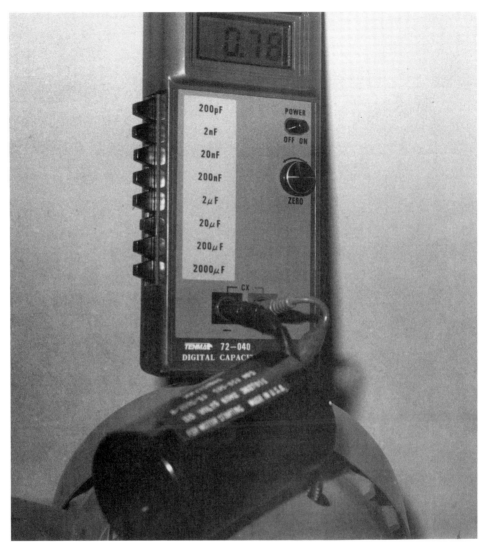

2-17 Check the motor capacitor with the small capacitor tester. For best results, remove one lead to the capacitor.

Chapter **3**

Motor basics

*T*he function of a motor is to transfer electrical energy into mechanical energy. The various motors contained in most power tools are: universal, split phase, capacitor, three-phase, and dc motors.

The universal motor is the most popular ac motor in smaller ac power tools (FIG. 3-1). The split-phase and capacitor start motors are found in larger power tools, while huge machines like commercial planers and molders use three-phase motors. Finally, the dc motor is used in cordless battery-operated power tools.

UNIVERSAL MOTOR

The universal motor is a series-wound motor from 0 to ¾ horsepower (FIG. 3-2). The universal motor contains field and armature coils, brushes, and the switch—wired in series (FIG. 3-3). The two brushes are 180° apart and provide current to the commutator, then to the armature windings. The universal motor may be operated on ac or dc power (FIG. 3-4). The speed of the motor may be controlled with a variable resistor, used in series with the other components (FIG. 3-5).

The universal motor brushes are held into position with radial holders and can slide in and out of these plastic or metal holders (FIG. 3-6). After several years of constant use the carbon-graphite material from the brushes builds up and prevents the motor from rotating. The brushes can stick in the holder and prevent current from passing on to the commutator and armature. Often, these brushes are spring loaded. Reverse the universal motor rotation by interchanging brush wires (FIG. 3-7). This shifts the brushes 180° from the original position (FIG. 3-8).

SPLIT-PHASE MOTOR

The split-phase induction motor is found in washing machines, fans, and pumps as well as power tools. In split-phase motors, the high starting torque is obtained by adding another starting winding to the main starter winding (FIG. 3-9). Often, the starting winding has a higher resistance and is wound in the same space as the starter. When the motor has reached 80 percent of its required speed, the starting switch opens and takes the starting winding out of the circuit (FIG. 3-10).

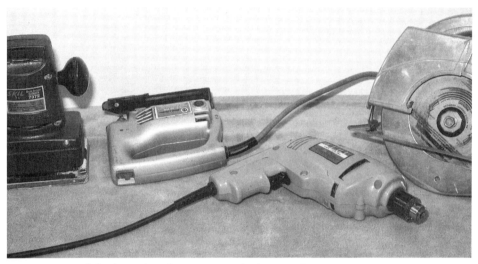

3-1 Several small power ac tools that contain universal motors.

3-2 Inside view of the universal motor. The main components are the brushes, field coil, armature, and commutator.

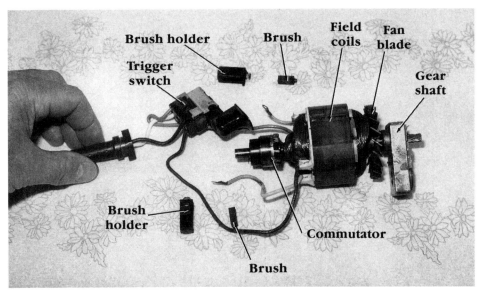

3-3 Field coils, brushes, armature, and switch are wired in series.

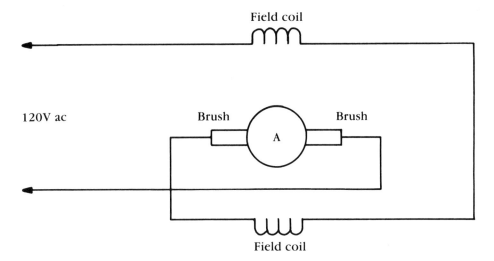

3-4 Schematic diagram of the universal motor, which may be operated on ac or dc power.

In this motor, the starting winding is wound on top of the main winding with small wire for additional resistance. The front of the motor is the bell end, which is opposite the motor shaft and pulley. Most split-phase motors run counterclockwise. The direction may be changed by switching the field wires of the main winding (FIG. 3-11). Check the resistance of the field coil to determine if open or shorted, or to isolate the main winding from the starting winding.

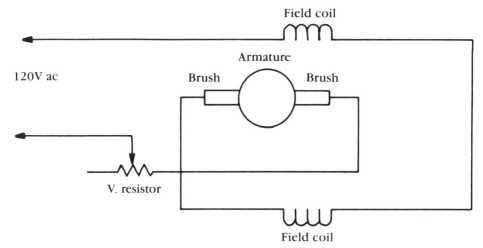

3-5 The speed of the universal motor may be controlled with a variable resistor in series with the other components.

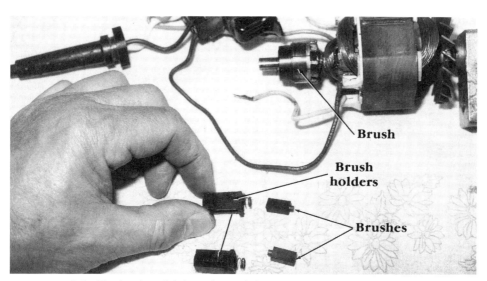

3-6 The brushes slide in and out of the metal or plastic brush holder.

CAPACITOR MOTOR

The capacitor motor is in the split-phase family of motors. The capacitor or condenser adds starting torque to the stator windings. It is usually located on top of the motor (FIG. 3-12), and is in series with the starting winding and switch (FIG. 3-13). When the capacitor motor reaches speed, the starting switch cuts out the capacitor and starting winding from the circuit. The capacitor start motor may be found on bench saws and small planers.

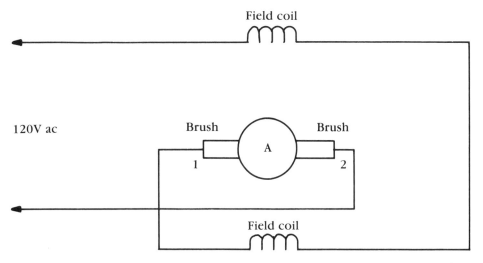

3-7 The universal motor rotation may be reversed by interchanging brush wires 1 and 2.

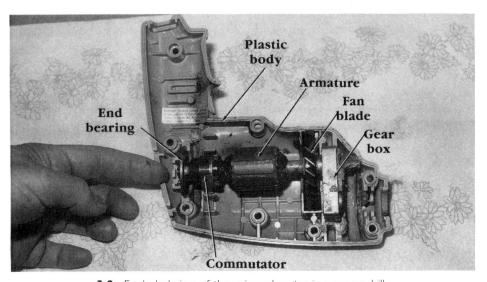

3-8 Exploded view of the universal motor in a power drill.

The capacitor

Capacitors used to be known as *condensers*. The capacitor used in motor start circuits is an electrolytic type. The capacity may vary from 70 to 650 microfarads, depending upon the horsepower of the motor. The electrolytic capacitor is made up of several layers of tin foil, with paste applied on the dielectric paper between windings.

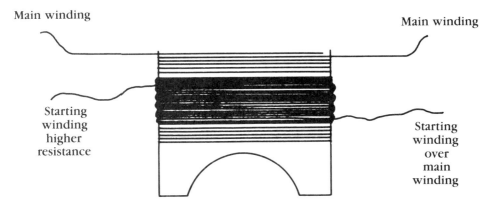

Main winding

Main winding

Starting
winding
higher
resistance

Starting
winding
over
main
winding

3-9   In a split-phase motor, high starting torque is obtained by adding a starting winding in the same slots as the main winding.

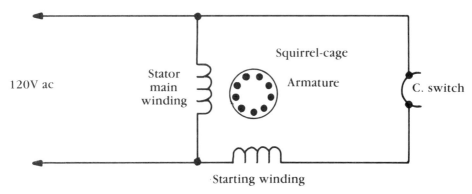

Squirrel-cage

120V ac

Stator
main
winding

Armature

C. switch

Starting winding

3-10   Schematic of a split-phase motor with starting switch and squirrel-cage armature. This armature has no coil windings.

Replace the motor capacitor with the same capacity and working voltage as the original. Suspect the capacitor, starting winding, or starting switch when the motor will not start up, or if the motor turns slowly or groans and hums. Check the suspected capacitor as follows.

First remove the cover of the capacitor. You can check the capacitor with the portable tester (FIG. 3-14), or simply by using a screwdriver (FIG. 3-15). Plug in the motor, then remove the motor plug. Place the screwdriver across the capacitor terminals. If there is no spark or very little, replace the starting capacitor.

DC MOTOR

Cordless power tools are operated by dc motors, which run on batteries (FIG. 3-16). The dc motor has powerful ceramic magnets instead of the field coil. The armature has the coil windings with a very small commutator (FIG. 3-17). A wiring diagram of the dc motor is shown in FIG. 3-18.

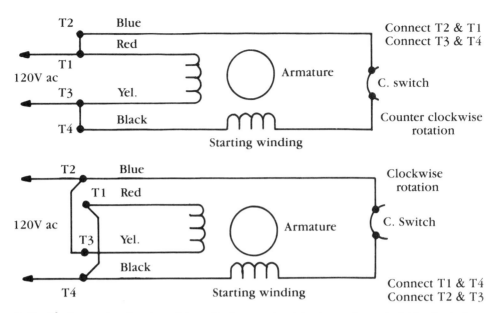

3-11 To change the direction of the split-phase motor, interchange the main field coil windings T1 and T3 (red and yellow).

3-12 The capacitor in the capacitor start motor is usually located on top of the motor. Replace the defective capacitor with one of same value and working voltage.

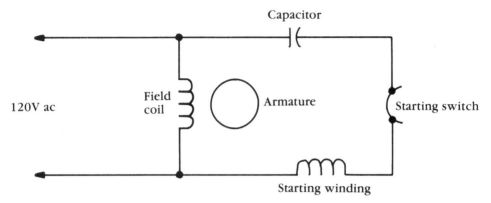

Capacitor

120V ac

Field
coil

Armature

Starting switch

Starting winding

3-13 Wiring diagram of the capacitor start motor. The starting switch takes the capacitor out of the circuit after the motor is up to speed.

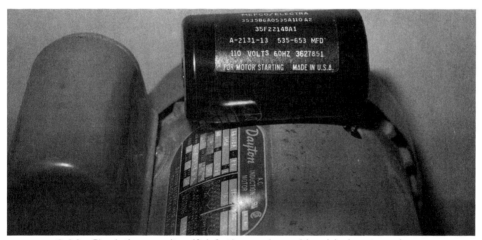

3-14 Check the capacitor. If defective, replace with original part number.

The dc motors in cordless tools may operate from 2.8- to 12-volt battery sources. Several nickel-cadmium batteries are wired in series to operate the tool (FIG. 3-19). The two-speed cordless tool may be operated on two batteries for the low speed and all five batteries for the high speed. The direction of the cordless tool is reversed by changing battery polarity at the motor terminals (FIG. 3-20).

Often a dc motor is cheaper to replace than to repair. However, try these steps if there are problems: Take the motor apart to clean up the commutator. Clean off both contact spring leaf brushes and commutator with cleaning fluid or alcohol and a cleaning stick. Check the armature windings with the ohmmeter. If the commutator is excessively burned or has deep arc pits, replace the motor. When replacing armature be careful not to damage commutator leaf type brushes (FIG. 3-21). Discard the motor if the bearings are extremely worn and noisy.

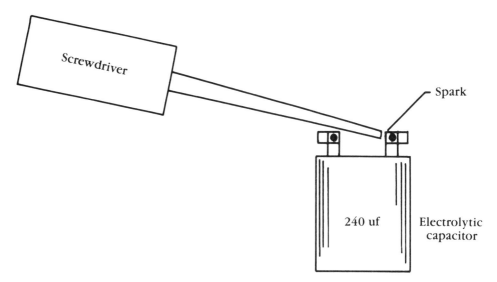

3-15 Always, discharge the capacitor before removing. The capacitor can also be checked by discharging with screwdriver. No charge or a weak charge might indicate a weak capacitor.

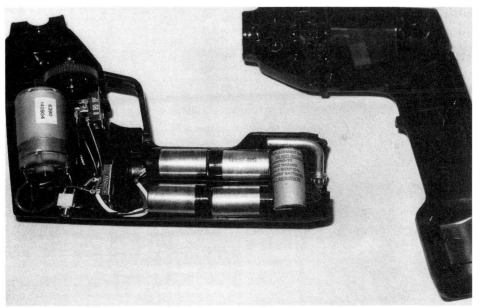

3-16 The cordless power tool with a battery-operated dc motor.

Two-phase, three-phase, or 220-volt motors are usually found in large commercial planers and sanders (FIG. 3-22). The current flows in all three windings. The three-phase motor has stator windings, which are fused at the control panel.

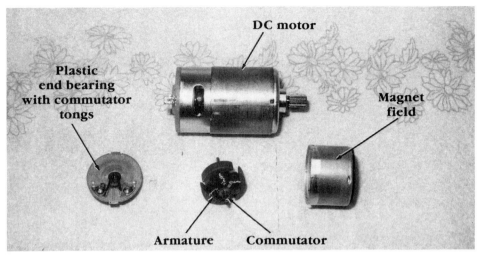

3-17   The small dc motor consists of a field magnet and armature with commutator. Notice the slip ring, prongs, or brushes that rotate the armature.

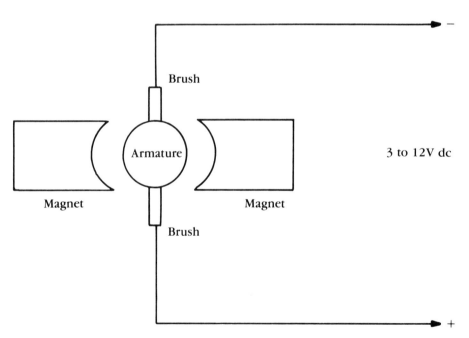

3-18   Schematic wiring of the dc motor, including brushes, commutator, armature winding, and PM magnets.

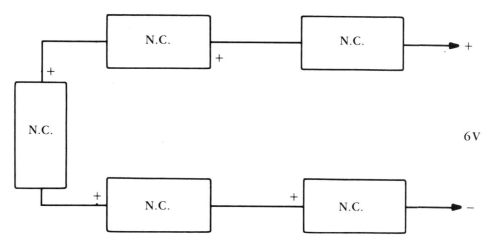

3-19 Several batteries are connected in series to power the dc motor in the cordless power tool.

6 V

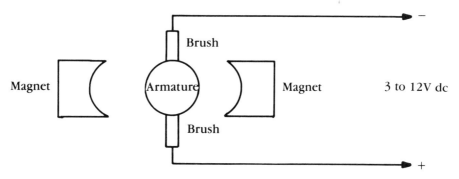

3-20 Reverse the dc motor by changing the battery polarity at the motor terminals.

3 to 12V dc

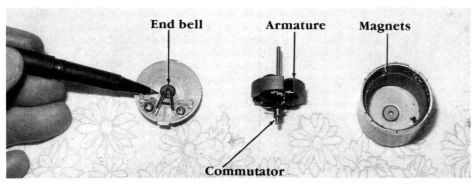

3-21 Inside view of the dc motor.

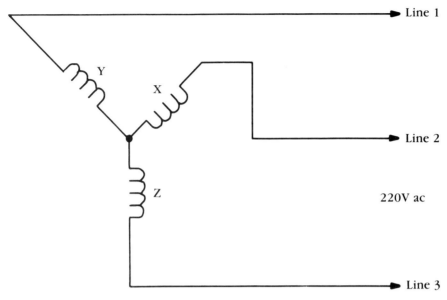

3-22 Schematic wiring of a large three-phase motor.

BRUSHES

The power tool motor brushes are made of carbon-graphite material. These brushes may be round or rectangular (FIG. 3-23). In small motors, brushes are radial or upright, and 180° apart on the commutator (FIG. 3-24). In larger motors, the brushes may lead at an angle to the commutator. These brushes have a small tension spring to apply pressure to the commutator.

Brushes carry the current to the commutator of the armature windings. Make sure the brushes aren't sticking in the holder and that the curvature of the brush is toward the round edge of the commutator. Wipe off the end of the brush that rides upon the commutator surface. It is important that the wire eyelet connecting the brush to the circuit is in place. On some brush holders the wire is soldered, on others it is held in place with a screw.

OVERLOAD PROTECTION

Some of the larger motors have a thermally activated cutout or circuit breaker consisting of a bimetallic disc with a resistance heater in the circuit (FIG. 3-25). When the motor begins to heat up after several hours of use, or overload is applied to the motor pulley, the heater will become warm and cause the bimetal disc to open the circuit. The bimetal strip deflects and opens contacts to the motor. The tool will shut off. In many cases you simply push a button on the motor to start it up again (FIG. 3-26).

Suspect an overloaded motor, binding bearings, or a defective motor when the overload cannot be reset after the motor cools down.

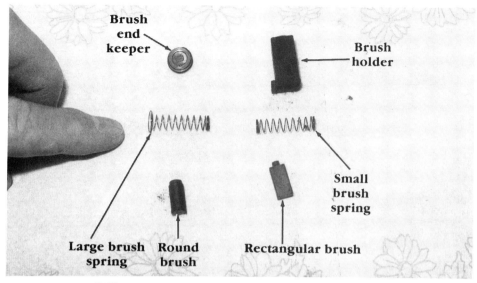

3-23 Various brushes found in universal and dc motors.

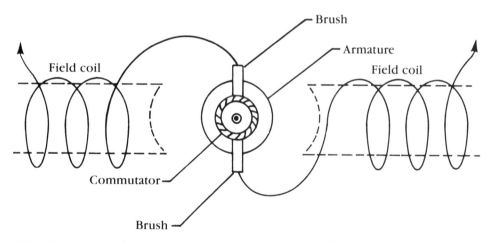

3-24 Brushes found in most universal motors are radial, or 180° apart, on the commutator.

STARTING SWITCH

When the motor reaches about 70 to 80 percent of its operating speed, a centrifugal force from the motor causes a slider on the shaft of the motor to be thrown, which disengages the starting switch. You can hear this switch disengage as the motor begins to reach its operating speed. When the motor is turned off, the switch will close again as the sliding device comes to rest near the rotor armature (FIG. 3-27).

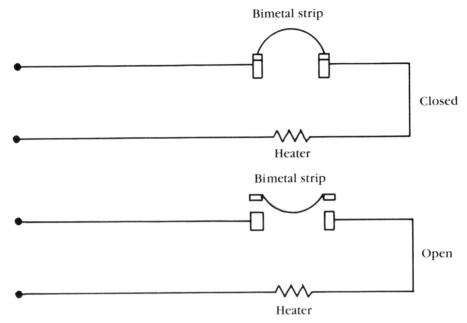

3-25 A relay or bimetallic cutout placed in one leg of the motor winding. The element heats up and causes bimetal strip to open the circuit.

Suspect dirty switch contacts when the motor does not start up, rotates slowly, or groans. The centrifugal switch may be broken or have dirty contacts, or the sliding cone on the motor shaft might not be sliding. Wash out switch contacts with cleaning solution and clean up the switch contacts.

Most starting switches are located inside the end bell of the motor, although on a few new motors the switch assembly might be on the outside of the motor.

BEARINGS

The motor can have bronze sleeve, ball bearing, or plastic bearings. Bronze bearings are common in most small power tools (FIG. 3-28), while ball bearings are found in larger motors. Plastic bearings sometimes contain ball bearings, and plastic sleeve bearings can be found in cordless power tool motors.

Bearings can freeze up or become excessively worn or dry. Adequate lubrication of the bearing prevents friction damage. Lubricate sleeve bearings with light oil, ball bearings with light grease or oil. When the motor is torn down for repair, wash out the bearings with cleaning fluid and lubricate before replacing.

ARMATURE

Inspect the commutator, being especially careful to notice broken soldered wires. It is also important that the surface of the commutator be clean and even. Dirty grooves may be repaired using sandpaper (FIG. 3-29). Rotate the armature, using a strip of sandpaper to clean and even up the surface. Deep grooves should be turned on the metal lathe or taken to a machine or motor repair shop. Do not use abrasive emery paper upon the commutator; particles might get down in the segments and short out the windings. Also keep oil and grease off of commutator. Check for broken armature wires with the ohmmeter (FIG. 3-30). Each coil winding should have equal resistance.

TROUBLESHOOTING MOTOR USING PIGTAIL LIGHT

A pigtail 25-watt light bulb with alligator clips may be used to check the motor. Clip the light across the ac wires that are connected to the motor to determine if 120 volts is being applied to the motor (FIG. 3-31). Place the pigtail light in series with motor winding to see if the field coil is open. Clip the pigtail light across the starting switch to see if contacts are good. If the light across the starting switch does not come on, the contacts are normal. The grounded motor is indicated by a dim light.

3-26   If the motor won't start or quits during operation, press the red overload button on motor assembly.

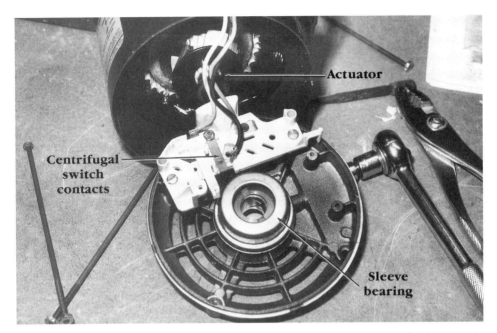

3-27 The centrifugal switch places the starting capacitor or winding in the circuit, then takes it out of the circuit when motor reaches speed.

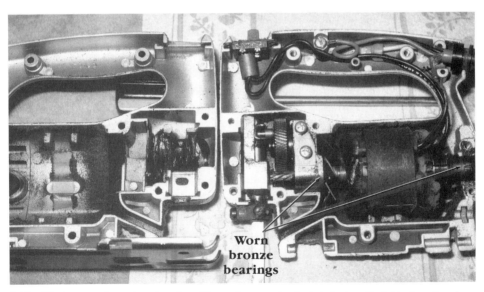

3-28 The bronze sleeve bearings found in small power tools. Lubricate with light oil and replace when excessively worn.

3-29 The brushes ride on the commutator, forming a slip ring motion. Keep the surface of the commutator clean and even.

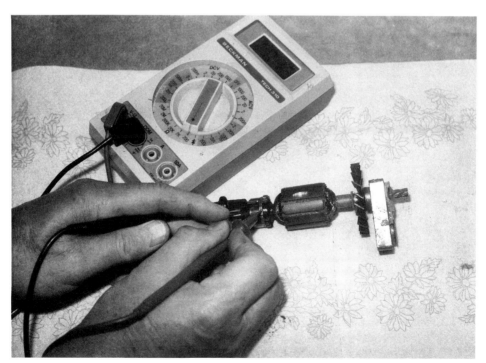

3-30 Check the armature coil windings with the ohmmeter. All windings should have about the same resistance.

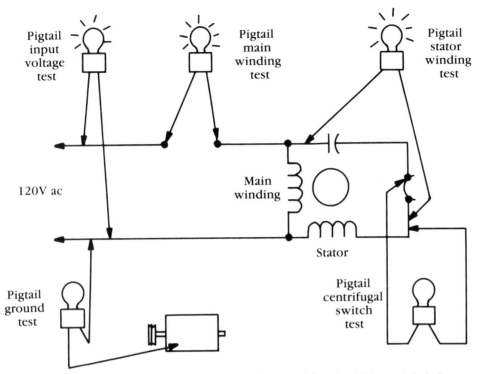

Pigtail input voltage test

Pigtail main winding test

Pigtail stator winding test

120V ac

Main winding

Stator

Pigtail ground test

Pigtail centrifugal switch test

3-31   Troubleshooting the suspected motor with a pigtail 25-watt light bulb.

WINDINGS

Check the continuity of a motor by connecting the ohmmeter to the motor terminals: A low resistance measurement indicates that motor continuity is fairly normal. If there is no measurement, suspect poor brushes, motor field coil, or
armature winding. Check each winding with the ohmmeter. The starting winding
of the capacitor or split-phase motor should have a higher resistance than the
main field winding.

Take a voltage measurement at the motor input terminals. A high voltage measurement across the motor cutout may indicate that the unit is defective and will
not reset. In universal or ac motors, take voltage measurements across each brush
to the other supply line to locate open field coils (FIG. 3-32). A grounded motor
might hum and groan. Measure the voltage from each each line terminal to the end
bell of the motor for grounded winding. If there is no reading, the motor should
be good. TABLE 3-1 gives troubleshooting tips for motors.

MARKING END BELLS

Before removing the end bell or shell of larger motors, mark each end with a
punch or chisel so you are sure to replace them properly (FIG. 3-33). Use a punch
because pen or pencil marks will wear off while handling or cleaning the motor.

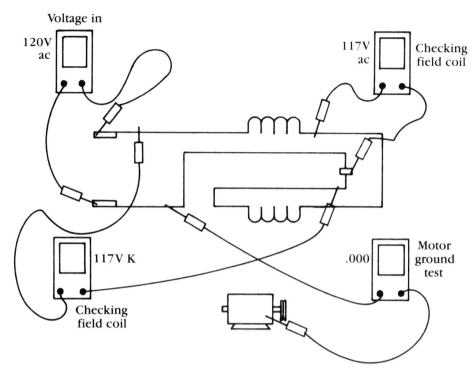

3-32 Take voltage measurements on the motor terminals, field coils, and shell of the motor to check for continuity and shorted field coil.

Table 3-1. Troubleshooting Chart for Motors

Problem	*Cause and Remedy*
Motor fails to start	1. Check voltage at the motor terminals
	2. Check for blown fuse
	3. Low voltage—check batteries on cordless power tools.
	4. Defective capacitor—replace
	5. Defective starting winding—check with ohmmeter for open
	6. Open motor circuit—check with ohmmeter
	7. Worn brushes—replace
	8. Frozen bearings—remove and replace
Motor stops in operation	1. Check for open thermal cutout
	2. Overheated motor—cool down
	3. Bearings frozen—wash out and lubricate
	4. Check for ground of motor field
	5. Low voltage at motor terminals
	6. Check for bad brushes
	7. Excessive load

Table 3-1. Continued.

Problem	*Cause and Remedy*
Motor does not come up to speed	1. Shorted field coil 2. Defective starting switch—replace 3. Defective capacitor—sub another 4. Motor overheats—cool for one hour 5. Dry bearings—wash out and lubricate 6. Excessive load 7. Check batteries in cordless motors
Excessive bearing wear	1. Belt too tight—adjust tension 2. Misaligned pulley—realign pulley 3. Dry bearings—lubricate 4. Dirty and gummed up bearings—wash out, clean up, lubricate 5. Overheated bearings—lubricate
Rotor rubs on stator	1. Dirt and sawdust in motor—clean out 2. Excessive worn bearings 3. Bent motor shaft
Motor overheats	1. Bad bearings—replace 2. Overworked—cool down 3. Shorted field coils—estimate for repair 4. Excessive load 5. Dry gear box—clean up and lubricate with light grease 6. Clean out vent holes 7. Needs lubrication 8. Excessive belt tension
Noisy motor	1. Worn bearings—replace 2. Rough commutator—turn down with metal lathe 3. Excessive end play—check for missing washer 4. Improper mounting 5. Bent motor shaft 6. Excessive dirt and dust in motor 7. Loose parts in or on motor
Excessive brush arcing	1. Dirty or worn commutator—clean up with sandpaper 2. Worn brushes—replace 3. Poor spring tension on brush—replace 4. Brush riding high 5. High mica—turn down with metal lathe 6. Oil on commutator—wash off and clean up

3-33 Before tearing the motor apart, punch two different sets of holes so you can fit the tool back together properly.

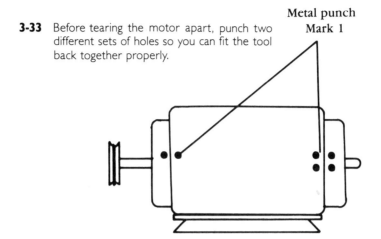

Metal punch
Mark 1

Chapter 4

Do-it-yourself repairs

Many small power tool repairs can be accomplished even by those unfamiliar with basic tools. A screwdriver, long-nose pliers, regular pliers, and a soldering gun are all that are needed for common repairs, and these tools are simple to use. With them you can repair or install power cords, ac plugs, switches, change brushes, and keep bearings lubricated. Simple repairs can help keep power tools running for many years. Refer to TABLE 4-1 for troubleshooting small power tools.

REPAIRING CORDS AND PLUGS

With age and use, the power cord of a tool becomes brittle, worn, or cut in places (FIG. 4-1). Damage can occur to or around the plug. In any of these cases, the plug and/or cord should be replaced.

The power cord often breaks at the plug or where it enters power tool. Simply cut off the power cord a couple of inches and install a new plug. Refer to FIGS. 4-2 through 4-4. Follow the electrical wiring code. Connect the green wire to the green terminal of the ground lug, the white wire to the silver brass terminal of the plug, the black wire to the bronze terminal. Make a hook in the wire and solder the scraped terminal wire so the connection will not pull out. Choose a rubber male plug instead of a plastic one for power cords. Remember to connect the ground terminal (FIG. 4-5).

CHECKING SWITCHES

Dead or intermittent operation might be the result of a defective switch, which in turn might be caused by dirty or burned contacts. Try to clean the dirty contacts by spraying cleaning fluid or silicone spray into the switch contacts. Work the switch back and forth to get cleaning fluid on the contacts. Replace the switch if it cannot be cleaned or has burned contacts.

Table 4-1. Troubleshooting Chart for Small Power Tools

Problem	*Cause and Remedy*
Motor won't start	1. Make sure tool is plugged in 2. Try another outlet 3. Check that safety switch is on 4. Check off/on trigger switch 5. Move speed switch to another setting 6. Change speed control 7. Check ac cord and plug 8. Check for worn brushes 9. Take continuity test of power tool
Tool does not rotate but motor is running	1. Check the belt tension on sander 2. Notice if belt is off or slipping 3. Check gear box for worn or broken gear 4. Check motor pulley
Sawdust in motor and power tool housing	1. Remove and clean 2. Insert vacuum nozzle in main housing 3. Take small motor apart and clean out all dust and dirt 4. Clean out air intake holes of motor with shop vacuum 5. Clean workplace
Noisy operation	1. Isolate motor to indicate if it is noisy 2. Check end bearings 3. Check large motor belt for slipping or worn areas 4. Inspect gear assembly for worn or dry gears
Motor smokes	1. Overworked motor—let it cool for one hour 2. Check the bearings for dry or gummed conditions 3. Motor winding might be shorted or grounded
Chuck does not tighten	1. Inspect chuck area for jammed or bent chuck assembly 2. Do not use pliers to tighten up chuck assembly 3. Check for loose or broken chuck fingers 4. See if all three holes will tighten with the chuck key

Use the ohmmeter to check for open or broken contacts. A good switch will indicate less than 1 ohm resistance between switch terminals. Replace the switch when the ohmmeter indicates more than 2 ohms between contacts. If the ohmmeter reading changes erratically when you simply touch the switch lever, this indicates a worn or burned switch terminal. Solder all switch contacts.

Replace a defective switch with the exact part number, if possible. Many small power tools use single-pole single-throw (SPST) or single-pole double-throw (SPDT) slide switches. These switches can be found at most electronic parts stores. The SPDT slide switches are used for motor speed switches.

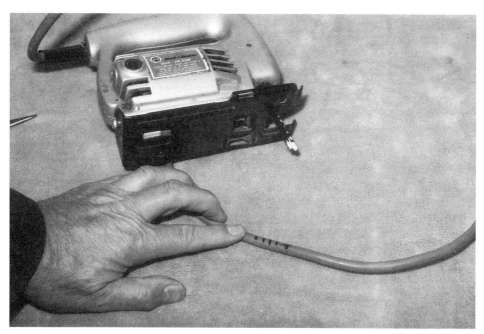

4-1 Check the power cord for cut, worn, or frayed areas. Replace the entire cord and plug with Number 18 or 16 wire.

4-2 Strip back the rubber cord, cut off filler material, and leave about 1½ inches free of the power cord.

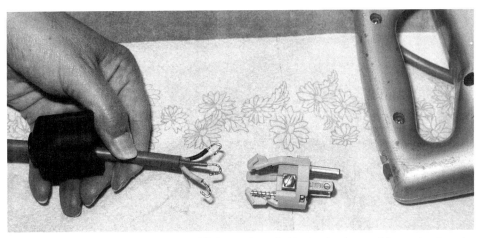

4-3   Twist the wire tightly and scrape it if it is not clean. Solder both wires and form a hook at the end.

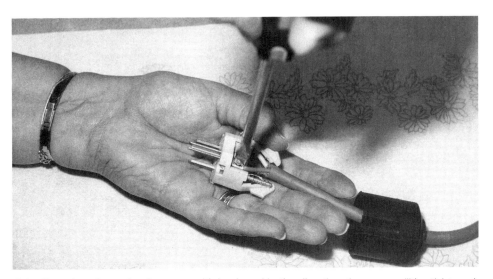

4-4   Place the wire under the screw with hook end in the direction the screw will be tightened.

MOTOR CONTINUITY TEST

Use the ohmmeter to check the motor continuity at the male plug. This will indicate whether the cord, brushes, or motor are open (FIG. 4-6). A normal power tool should show a low resistance between 10 and 25 ohms. It's best to use alligator clips to connect the ohmmeter to the ac plug terminals, so you can use your hand to rotate the motor or operate the on/off switch.

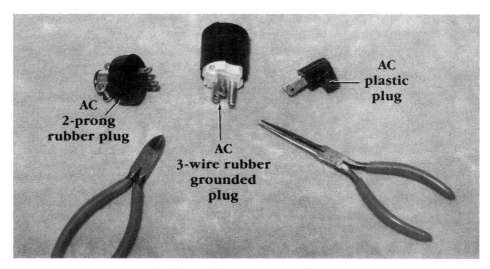

4-5 Three different types of male plugs.

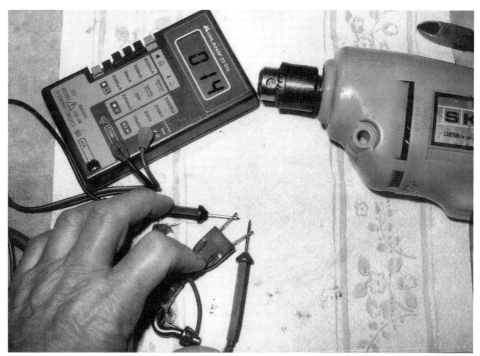

4-6 Check the motor continuity, cord, and switch at the male plug. The normal resistance should be between 10 and 25 ohms.

Suspect a dirty or defective switch if the meter shows an erratic or intermittent reading when the switch is triggered. Replace the defective switch. Flex the ac cord. If the measurement changes, check for a break in the wiring of the cord.

Rotate the drill chuck. If the ohmmeter reading becomes intermittent, suspect bad or worn brushes. No measurement at all might indicate an open brush or field coil winding (FIG. 4-7).

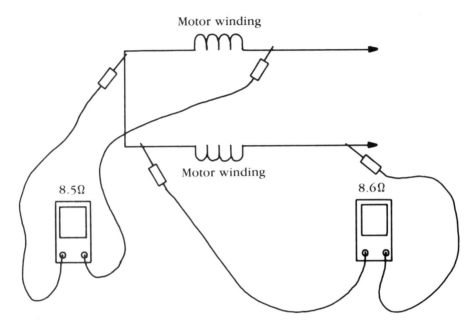

4-7   Use the ohmmeter to check the motor field continuity at one brush and at the off/on switch.

REPLACING MOTOR BRUSHES

It is not difficult to replace motor brushes. On many tools, you can simply remove a couple of screws and pull off the back plate of the motor to reach the brush holders (FIG. 4-8). On other power tools, the top cover must be removed and the brush holder unscrewed to reach the brushes (FIG. 4-9). Clean off the commutator and replace the brushes.

Check the motor brushes for excessive wear. If the brush is arcing excessively replace it. The brush may be worn down to practically nothing, which will result in a dead motor. Wipe off the commutator and brushes with cloth dampened with cleaning fluid. The brush can only be seated in one direction and must fit into the brush holder. Make sure the brush spring and terminal eyelet are in place. The brush should spring tightly against the motor armature.

4-8 On some power tools you need to simply remove the back cover to get at the brushes. Inspect the brushes for worn or improper seating.

4-9 Release one insulated screw to remove the brush holder in enclosed motors. Clean off the commutator and replace the new brush.

TEMPORARY SWITCHES

When replacing switches, the new one should be the same or approximately the same size as the old (FIG. 4-10). Check the amperage of the defective motor switches. Small power tools are rated at 2.5 amps, while larger tools may draw 8 to 10 amps. The switch replacement must have the same or higher amperage, or it will soon burn the switch contacts.

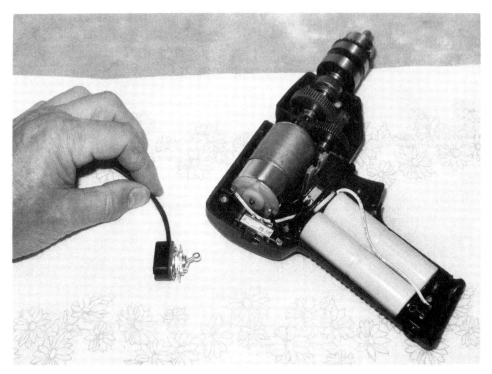

4-10   The defective slide switch can be replaced with another electronic slide or toggle switch. Make sure the new switch has the same or higher amperage rating.

Electronic slide or toggle switches may be substituted for the original on/off switches. A larger hole and washers might be needed to mount the toggle switch. If room is unavailable to mount the toggle switch, it may be mounted elsewhere—on the handle, for example. If the original or substitute switch cannot be placed, insert an on/off switch in the power cord (FIG. 4-11).

INSTALLING BENCH SWITCHES

You can install switches in your workbench. Use a standard variety and connect it to a single outlet. Simply solder the switch wiring terminals together, so the power tool is actually turned to on all the time, with the power controlled from a bench outlet (FIG. 4-12).

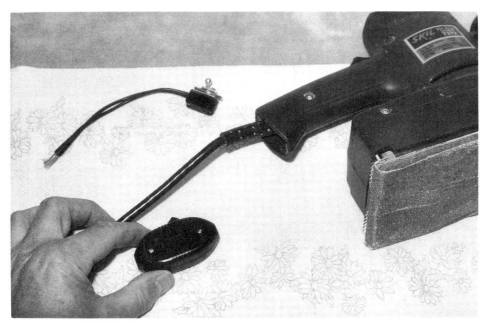

4-11   The temporary switch may be placed in the power cord. Solder the two original switch leads together.

4-12   Mount the ac receptacle with on/off switch into the workbench.

The bench outlet may also be used for larger power tools. Simply wire the switch in series with the power tool cord (FIG. 4-13).

CHECKING BEARINGS

Bronze sleeve bearings are found in most small power tools, at both ends of the motor armature. Reduction gear assemblies may have bronze sleeve or ball bearings (FIG. 4-14).

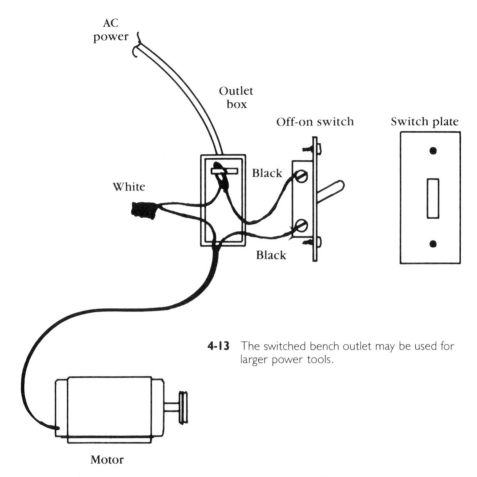

AC power

Outlet box

Off-on switch

Switch plate

White

Black

Black

Motor

4-13 The switched bench outlet may be used for larger power tools.

Inspect the bearings for worn areas or missing ball bearings. Sleeve bronze end bearings can become worn, dry, or frozen (FIG. 4-15). Notice if the armature shaft vibrates or has some play inside the bronze bearings. Check if the shaft can be moved side to side. Poor bearings can become noisy, vibrate, and freeze up—slowing down the motor speed.

First wash faulty ball bearings with solvent or mineral oil, then lubricate. Also check the bearing ring for a missing ball (FIG. 4-16). Sometimes the ring becomes worn and one or two balls may drop out. Be careful not to lose small ball bearings when replacing. If they do get lost, check the manufacturer's parts list, service depot, or the local motor repairman for sleeve or ball bearing replacement.

LUBRICATION

Follow the manufacturer's operation manual for correct lubrication of power tools. Sleeve bearings should be lubricated with a light motor oil, 3-in-1 oil, multipurpose lubricant, or silicone lubricant spray (FIG. 4-17).

4-14 The bronze sleeve bearing is found at both ends of the motor armature.

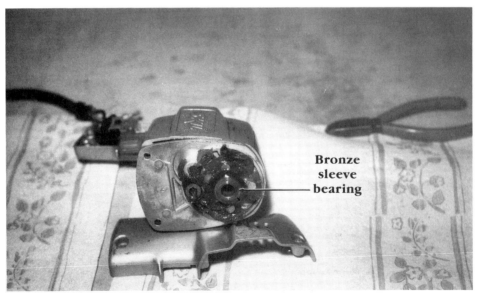

4-15 The bronze sleeve bearing may be worn, dry, or frozen.

4-16 Wash out the ball bearings with solvent or mineral oil, then apply light oil or grease on the ball bearing assembly.

4-17 Lubricate bearings with Number 10 or 20 SAE motor oil, 3-in-1 oil, multi-lubricant, or silicone lubricant spray.

Bearings that are squeaky or noisy probably require lubrication. If bearings are frozen, use WD-40 or carburetor cleaner to release the sleeve bearing. Look for oil well holes at the end of the motor assembly (FIG. 4-18). Apply light grease or oil when replacing or lubricating the ball bearing assembly.

4-18 Check the end bell or motor assembly for an oil well or hole for lubricating the armature bearings.

BROKEN HOOKUP WIRES

Because of continual vibration during use, connecting wires inside the motor of a power tool can break off and make the tool inoperative. Take a continuity resistance measurement at the ac cord with the switch turned on. After checking cord and plug, remove the cover from the tool and visually inspect the connections. Check the small plastic twist connections for poor or open connections, and inspect the switch for poorly soldered or broken connections (FIG. 4-19). Also check that the wires connected to the brush terminals are intact.

CHECKING FIELD COILS

Use the ohmmeter to check the motor for open or burned field coils (FIG. 4-20). Often, the field coils are in series with the brushes or ac switch. A shorted field coil can cause the armature to rotate slowly, hum, or vibrate. If the coils of small motors are burned or charred, the motor is not worth fixing. Take large motors with burned windings to a repairman for an estimate.

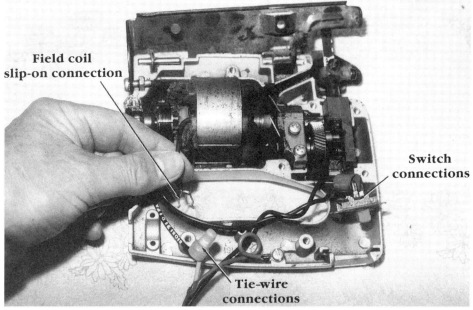

Field coil slip-on connection

Switch connections

Tie-wire connections

4-19 Check the switch, plastic twist connectors, and brush wire terminals for poor or broken connecting wires.

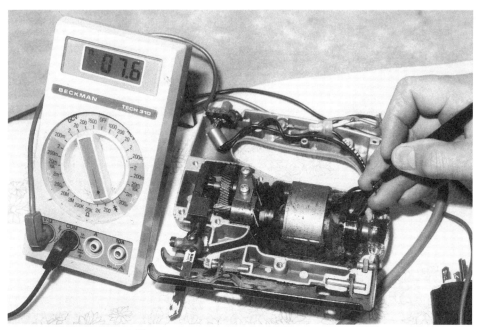

4-20 Check the field coils with the ohmmeter.

CHECKING THE ARMATURE

Excessive arcing of the brushes might indicate worn brushes, a dirty commutator, or that mica strips are running high on the commutator. Sometimes the motor will idle, arc, and sputter. Inspect the brushes. Pull the armature out if the brushes appear normal. Inspect the commutator for worn or burned marks (FIG. 4-21).

4-21 Inspect the commutator of the armature for worn or arcing areas.

The commutator copper segments must be turned down on a metal lathe if excessively worn or if the mica between the copper segments are high. If a metal lathe is not handy, take the armature to a metal machine or motor repair shop.

If the commutator needs to be cleaned, run very fine sandpaper over the rotating armature. (Do not use emery paper; the particles can collect in the slots and short out the coil segments.)

Check the continuity of the armature coil windings in case a wire is broken off (FIG. 4-22).

VIBRATION

Excessive power tool vibration can be caused by a defective bearing, loose flywheel, or defective belt. On large power tools, such as bench saws, planers, and molders, remove the belt to find the source of the vibration. Replace worn, lumpy, or torn belts (FIG. 4-23). On orbital sanders, a loose flywheel can increase vibrations. Loose metal laminations also have a tendency to vibrate.

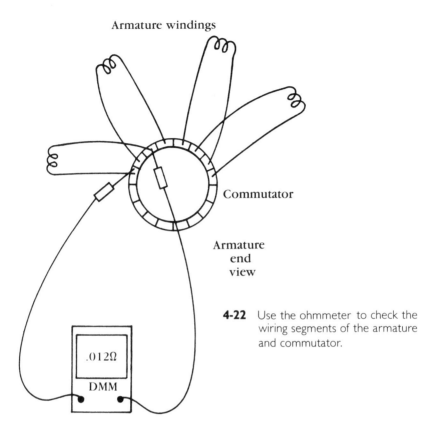

Armature windings

Commutator

Armature
end
view

4-22 Use the ohmmeter to check the wiring segments of the armature and commutator.

.012Ω

DMM

REPAIRING PLASTIC BODIES

Most power tools today have plastic impact covers that will not crack or break when dropped. However, older power tools might have breakable plastic bodies. You can repair these broken areas with fiberglass patching or auto repair kits (FIG. 4-24).

Fill the area to be repaired with foam spray or wrapped paper. Place a layer of filler or fiberglass over the area and let the material set up. Smooth the second layer out, contoured to the tool body, and let this set up overnight. Sand down the patched area and spray two coats of auto enamel over whole plastic body. The tool will look as good as new.

WHEN TO DISCARD A TOOL

It often costs more to repair defective small power tools than to replace them. Larger power tools, however, are probably cheaper to repair than replace. When bearings or parts cannot be found to repair the power tool, you will have to replace it. Sometimes parts are impossible to find because the tool is old and out of production.

4-23   A worn or cracked belt can cause the power tool to slip or vibrate.

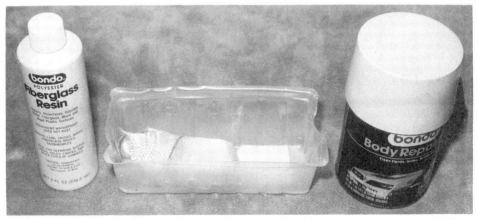

4-24   Repair broken handles or body areas of power tools with fiberglass kits or auto body filler.

WHEN TO CALL A PROFESSIONAL

Call a professional when you feel you cannot repair a power tool safely. Small power tools can usually be taken back to the manufacturer's repair depot or small appliance repair shop. Always check the warranty of a power tool and return it to the manufacturer's service centers if still under warranty. Do not break the power tool seals if the tool is under warranty.

Always ask for a repair estimate when taking a tool to the manufacturer's service center or local appliance repair shop. The owner's manual should list service centers.

Chapter **5**

Cleanup and lubrication

Power tools can last a lifetime if properly cared for, cleaned, and maintained. Wipe each power tool after use. Periodic checkups help prevent major problems and keep tools in good working condition. The exterior and interior areas of tools should be free of excessive grease, water, dirt, dust, and oil. Wipe off all metal surfaces with a dab of oil or a soft cloth to prevent rust.

GENERAL CLEANUP

Keep the work area clean and uncluttered. Keep all power tools as clean as possible. A shop vacuum is a valuable piece of equipment that can be used to clean tools and the work area (FIG. 5-1). Cleaning power tools and motors prevents them from becoming plugged with dirt and dust. Some power tools have vacuum attachments.

First vacuum up all dust and dirt. Then clean exteriors of portable power tools with soap and water. Because many portable tools have plastic housings, chemicals could damage the plastic sides. Do not use chlorinated cleaning solvents or household detergents that contain ammonia on plastic. Use an old toothbrush and a 2-inch paintbrush to clean in crevices. Keep water out of motor port holes. Avoid using cleaning fluid and solvents with small portable tools.

In the past, carbon tet (carbon tetrachloride), gasoline, or kerosene were used to clean motors and tools. These solvents are toxic and flammable, and are best avoided. If you do use them, go outside or to a well-ventilated area. A spark from a tool or furnace may cause these solvents to explode or start a fire. Keep all solvents away from motor windings. Use caution with all these types of cleaning agents, and follow the manufacturer's suggested procedures.

Every three months or so, clean out the motor vent holes to keep motor cool and to prevent overheating.

5-1   The wet/dry shop vac.

PERIODIC CHECKUPS

All power tools used over 100 hours per year should have an annual checkup. This is especially true of the large motors found in shapers, planers, and sanders. Check the motor bearings for dry, defective, or worn bearings. Check lubrication of bearings on large motors and rotating devices at least once a year (FIG. 5-2).

Check small portable power tools for excessive firing at the brushes. The brushes might be worn down, have oil dripping down on the armature, or have excessive dust on the commutator. Inspect the bearings. Check the power cord for cracked or broken areas. Inspect the ac plug for bent or broken prongs. Make sure that the grounding prong is still intact. Use the ohmmeter to take a ground continuity test between the ground plug and metal area of the power tool (FIG. 5-3). Notice if any part of the plastic housing is cracked or broken.

Brush out all dirt and dust from motor housing, then suck it up with the shop vacuum. Wash the plastic housing of power tools. Scrape off old chipped paint. Scrub and clean off all rust from metal areas. A touch up with spray paint prevents rust and can make the power tool look like new again. Polish or buff off the metal areas of the portable tools, then wipe them off with a dab of oil on a soft cloth. Periodic cleanups help keep power tools running longer (TABLE 5-1). You can also take power tools to the manufacturer's service center for checkups, if you prefer.

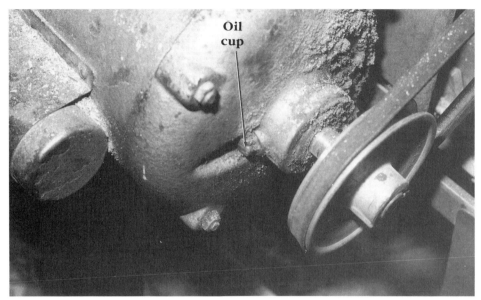

5-2 Dirt and dust that collects on the table saw should be cleaned at least once a year.

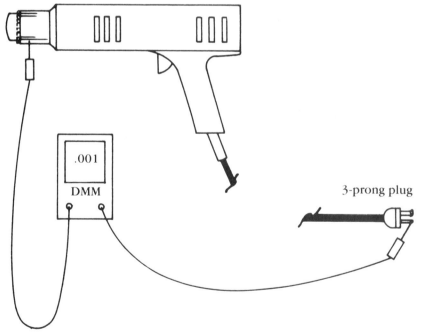

5-3 Make sure the power tool is grounded. Take a resistance check between ground terminal and metal areas on the motor.

Table 5-1. Periodic Checkups for Power Tools

Check	*100 Hours*	*6 Months*	*1 Year*
1. Plug and cord	x	x	x
2. Switches	x	x	x
3. Clean switch contacts	x		x
4. Oil bearings	x	x	x
5. Grease bearings	x	x	x
6. Motor brushes	x	x	x
7. Motor bearings	x	x	x
8. Cleanup	x	x	x
9. Rust forming		x	x
10. Check ac receptacle			x
11. Tighten bolts and nuts	x		x
12. Noisy conditions	x	x	x
13. Motor belts	x	x	x
14. Motor reset button			x
15. Motor capacitor			x

LUBRICATION

Many new portable power tools have been lubricated and greased at the factory, and don't need attention again for at least one or two years. Some have lifetime greased bearings. Of course, if the bearing becomes noisy or dry, it needs lubrication. Light machine oil or 3-in-1 oil will do the job.

If the gears seem excessively noisy, they might require extra grease. The lubrication the power tool needs depends on how it is used. Check the manufacturer's literature on lubricating.

Check the small power tool bearings at least once a year. A drop of Number 10 or 20 SAE motor oil can be applied through the small oil holes (FIG. 5-4). Some power tools have oil holes at the end of the tool for lubricating. Defective, dry, or worn bearings can cause the power tool to slow down, or damage the bearings and the motor. Apply a light oil to bronze sleeve bearings, light grease to ball bearings.

In larger motors, the ball or roller bearings are packed with grease. Check the grease fittings. For some, a hand grease gun is used to replace the old grease. Use only a high-grade grease with a high melting point for ball bearings.

Large motors might have sleeve bearings with oil cups or wells at each end of the motor. Fill up the well or cup halfway. If there is only a hole in which to place oil, use only a squirt or two. Do not use too much oil; it can drip on the field winding, destroy wire insulation, and cause breakdown of the field coil.

5-4 Place a drop of Number 10 or 20 SAE oil, or 3-in-1 oil in the small oil hole to prevent worn sleeve bearings.

Small power tools might not have any lubrication openings. In this case, the cover must be removed to oil the tool. Use light oil or grease on the bearings. Use a light mineral or machine oil, or Number 10 or 20 SAE motor oil for lubrication of sleeve bearings. Silicone oil spray may be used on moving levers, screw shafts, and adjustment assemblies. Check the manufacturer's literature for correct types of oil.

Gear box lubrication

The gear box or case in some small hand tools are lubricated at the factory and should not require additional lubrication (FIG. 5-5). If the gear box is excessively noisy or jammed, apply fresh lubricant to the gear assembly. Suspect dry gears and bearings if the motor shaft or chuck rotates very slowly or not at all. Check for a jammed gear box if the motor hums and groans without any rotation. Apply WD-40, Liquid Wrench, or silicone spray for jammed gears, frozen motor bearings, and rusty bolts.

RUST PREVENTION

Most power tools will show some signs of rust when stored in an outside garage or unheated workshop, or in areas of the country with high humidity. If possible, keep the workshop at an even temperature and provide adequate ventilation to help prevent rust from forming on power tools.

Test the shop area by scattering a few metal finishing nails. If they begin to rust in three months, you have a temperature, humidity, or ventilation problem. Wipe the metal surface of power tools with a light film of oil to prevent rust from forming.

Gear box

5-5 Some gear boxes in power tools are lubricated for life at the factory. This power drill has air-cooled permanently lubricated gears, ball thrust, and sleeve bearings for longer life.

5-6 Excessive rust can be removed with a few solvents and elbow grease.

Metal table maintenance

The tops on cabinets, tables, or bench-top saws can be made of light formed metal, aluminum, plastic, or cast iron. To prevent a metal table from rusting, apply a light film of oil or silicone spray.

If the table is already rusty in spots, use a rust cleaner or solvent (FIG. 5-6). Remove excess rust with a circular metal brush, then use the cleaner. Finish the area with fine abrasive paper. Finally, apply light coat of silicone oil spray upon the whole table.

SHOP VACUUM REPAIR

Check the cord, switch and wiring when the shop vac will not start up (FIG. 5-7). Inspect the cord for breakage when intermittent operation is the problem. Keep filters changed to prevent motor damage. Check hose and vents when the unit will not pick up dry materials. Following are pointers for vacuum use:

- Do not pick up explosive dust like coal, grain, or other combustible materials.
- Use a three-wire grounding extension cord to reach long distances from the outlet. Do not cut off the ground terminal.
- Do keep the filter changed to prevent motor damage. Wash filters out with soapy water.
- Wear goggles or keep eyes away from the air discharge path.
- Shut off vacuum when it tips over. This will allow the floating ball to resume an upright position.
- Do not use the machine to pick up gasoline or kerosene spills.
- Wash out tank and hose after a wet cleanup.

To repair, remove screws to dismount the motor from the front cover (FIG. 5-8). Remove fan blade assembly to get at motor (FIG. 5-9). Check the motor brushes and windings for poor or bad connections (FIG. 5-10). While the motor is open, inspect both motor bearings (FIG. 5-11).

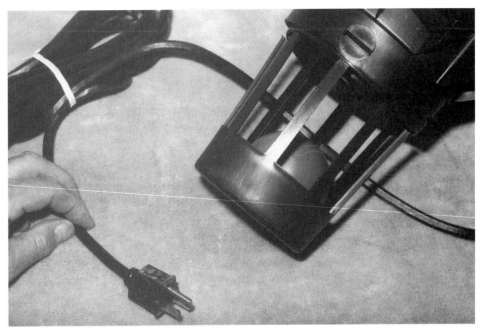

5-7 Inspect the cord, plug, and switch on the shop vac.

5-8 Remove external screws to dismount the motor assembly from top cover.

5-9 Remove the blade assembly of the shop vac to get at the motor.

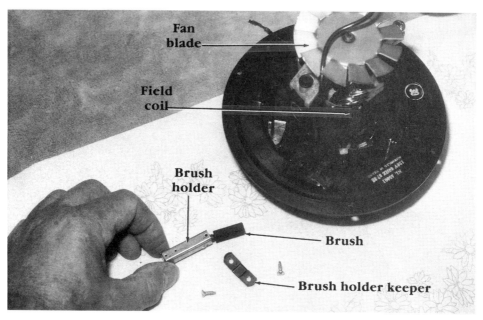

5-10 Check the motor brushes for excessive firing or worn areas.

5-11   Take a continuity check when the motor will not rotate. Inspect brushes and cord where it enters the shop cleaner.

Chapter **6**

Cordless battery-operated tools

Cordless power tools can be used practically anywhere. They have no cords to dangle or trip over (FIG. 6-1). The cordless power tool operates from a nickel-cadmium battery, which is usually contained in the handle of the cordless tool. The tool may operate several hours before a charge is needed, and it can be charged up in 1 to 3 hours.

Nickel-cadmium batteries are found in many household products. They are used in small hand mixers, radios, and cordless telephones, as well as in more powerful tools such as cordless drills, screwdrivers, drill drivers, reversing angle drills, and saws.

The cordless drill, reversing angle drill, and sander operate from a 7.2-volt battery, while the jigsaw, reciprocating saw, drill driver, and circular saw usually operate from a 9.6-volt source. Some heavy-duty circular saws operate from a 10.8-volt dc battery source. The voltage range for cordless tool batteries falls between 7.2 and 12 volts dc (TABLE 6-1).

SAFETY

All cordless power tools come with their own charging power source. Do not use any other battery charger than the one that comes with the tool. If the charger does not have the correct voltage, damage to the drill or battery may result and create a hazardous condition.

Do not store the charger and drill in areas where the temperature exceeds 120° Fahrenheit. Charge the battery in moderate temperatures; it will not charge properly if extremely cold or hot. Do not expose charger to rain, snow, or damp weather.

6-1   Cordless power tools have no dangling cords and come in all sizes and shapes.

**Table 6-1. Battery Voltages of
Selected Cordless Power Tools**

Tool	Battery Voltage
Skil 2105 Cordless Screwdriver	2.9 V dc
Menards 241-1011 Cordless Drill/Driver	4.8 V dc
Black & Decker 9020 ³/₈-inch Cordless Drill	7.2 V dc
Makita 9035DW Finishing Sander	7.2 V dc
Roybi BD101R Reversing Drill	7.2 V dc
Makita 4300DW Cordless Jig Saw	9.6 V dc
Makita 6500DW Circular Saw	10.8 V dc

Remember, battery tools are always ready for operation. Keep the trigger lock in the off position when not using the power tool. Do not run drill or tool while it is plugged into the charging unit.

Note: Be extremely careful when using any drill or saw through concealed walls to avoid contact with hot electrical wires. Hold the drill by the plastic handle only, and do not place the other hand on metal pipes, furnace ducts, or metal plumbing. Keep your hands away from the metal parts of the drill.

Wrap defective batteries in newspaper and place in the garbage. Do not throw the batteries in a fire; they could explode and cause bodily damage. Likewise, do not store batteries near a fire or excessive heat.

Sometimes you might notice liquid draining from the battery cells. This can occur from heavy use or hot temperatures. Usually, however, the battery seal must be broken before the liquid leaks out. If you come in contact with this liquid, wash your hands with soap and water, then apply lemon juice or vinegar. Do not touch your eyes. If the liquid gets in your eyes, wash out with clear water and call your doctor or the emergency room.

CHARGING BATTERIES

Some power tools have two or more nickel-cadmium rechargeable batteries. Remember, reduce the risk of injury by charging only nickel-cadmium type chargeable batteries. If you attempt to charge any non-chargeable battery, it could explode and cause injuries and excessive damage.

Charge the battery right after purchasing a new cordless power tool. Usually, the battery will not charge up to full capacity the first few times. After repeated use, the batteries for a cordless tool will receive a full charge. Most nickel-cadmium batteries charge in 3 to 4 hours. The batteries may be charged several thousand times before they wear out.

Charge the battery when the power tool will not operate or slows down to a crawl. Do not keep using it, until it is completely dead: this could short out the battery terminals and drain the battery. Do not be alarmed if the charger begins to hum or get warm while charging up the batteries.

If the power tool has not been used for 3 months or longer, the battery should be charged for 3 to 5 hours.

Defective charger or battery

If the battery quits before the normal operating time is up, suspect a defective battery or improper charging. Do not recharge the battery after using it for only a few minutes. Sometimes the batteries will build up a resistance before reaching a full charge, which reduces the operating time of the tool.

Check the power outlet or charger when the batteries will not charge properly. Inspect the jack on the power tool for bad connections. Has the power tool been in excessive heat or cold conditions during charging? Feel the body of the charger; it should be warm after a couple hours of charging. Suspect a defective charger or cord if the battery does not charge up. Check the output voltage of the charger. If normal, suspect a defective battery. Often, a defective or weak battery will not hold the charge long.

BATTERY REPLACEMENT

When the battery has been used for several years and will not take a charge, it must be replaced. You can replace it yourself or take it to the nearest service center. If the tool is still under warranty, do not touch it. Take the tool or send it to the authorized service center for repair.

The cordless tool must be disassembled to gain access to the built-in battery, which is usually in the handle of the power tool (FIG. 6-2). Take off the plastic casing by carefully removing the recessed screws. Lay the tool flat before removing the cover so bearings and gears do not fall out of place.

6-2 Remove the top cover to get at the batteries. The bottom might have to be unsoldered or clipped from the circuit.

Once the casing is removed, you will find the two different batteries that operate the tool, here a cordless drill (FIG. 6-3). These batteries are much heavier than flashlight batteries. Notice the top and bottom terminal wires are soldered to the battery.

In this two-speed drill, five different nickel-cadmium batteries operate the tool (FIG. 6-4). The 6-volt dc source provides a 200 and 500 RPM operation; different batteries are switched into the circuit by the speed switch. The trigger finger switch provides the different speeds while the switch at the top of the trigger area provides reverse speed. Note that here slip-on rather than soldered connectors release the battery terminals.

When replacing defective batteries, the whole pack should be removed and replaced. Most battery terminals are welded together for good inter-terminal connections. Suspect poorly soldered or broken terminal connections if the tool won't operate, or operates slowly. Take the battery pack with model number to a service center for replacement. Remember, the center terminal of these nickel-cadmium batteries is positive and the metal case is negative.

6-3 Two separate nickel-cadmium batteries operate this power tool.

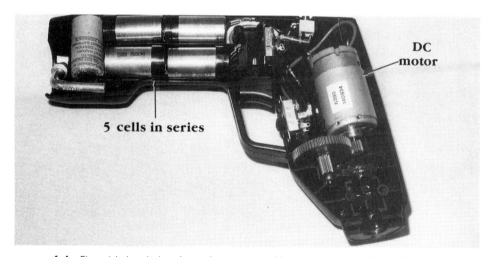

6-4 Five nickel-cadmium batteries connected in series operate this cordless drill.

CIRCUITS

All cordless power tools use a dc motor. The size of the motor depends upon the job for which the power tool is designed. A two-speed cordless tool operates at two different voltages. A reversible tool works by simply reversing the polarity of the battery at the dc motor terminals (FIG. 6-5).

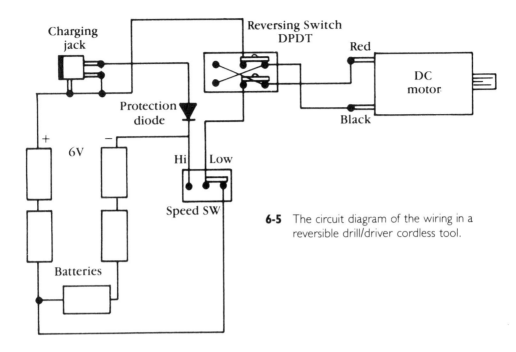

6-5 The circuit diagram of the wiring in a reversible drill/driver cordless tool.

In this model, the reverse switch is located above the trigger guard and off/on switch. A separate speed switch injects a higher or lower voltage from the battery by switching the different negative voltage to the reverse switch and on to the motor terminals. Notice the charging jack is wired directly at both total battery terminals.

Most dc motors are wired in the same manner. This two-speed cordless drill with a polarity diode and separate reversing switch is an exception (FIG. 6-6). The polarity diode in the positive leg of the charging jack prevents a different polarity of voltage from occurring at the jack. Besides polarity charge protection, the small diode prevents battery voltage feedback to the charging outlet jack.

Both the reversing and speed switches are separate components. The double-pole double-throw (DPDT) reversing switch reverses the motor for forward and reverse operations by applying an opposite voltage to the motor terminals. The single-pole single-throw (SPST) two-speed switch applies the entire battery voltage for high speed (500 RPM) and lower voltage for the slow speed (200 RPM). All five batteries are in series for 6-volt operation.

THE CHARGER

Measure the voltage of the charger at the cord output plug. You will find the voltage measured is higher than the total voltage of the batteries, or the voltage listed upon the charger. TABLE 6-2 lists operating and charging voltages. If the voltage is low or nonexistent, suspect a defective charger.

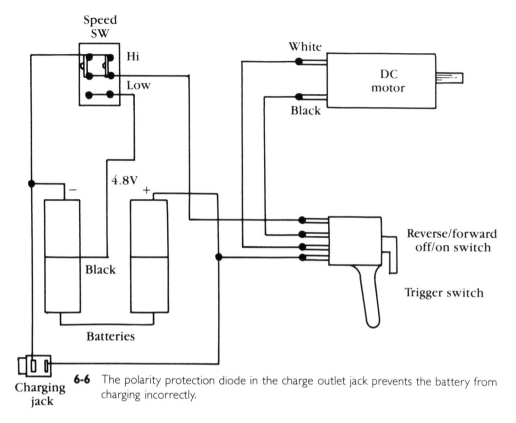

6-6 The polarity protection diode in the charge outlet jack prevents the battery from charging incorrectly.

**Table 6-2. Operating vs. Charging
Voltages of Selected Cordless Power Tools**

Tool	Operating Voltage	Charging Voltage
Skil Cordless 2105 Screwdriver	2.9 V	3.48 V
Dremel 850/8500 Drill Kit	7.5 V ac	9.67 V ac
Black and Decker 920 Cordless Drill	7.5 V dc	9.65 V dc
Menards 241-1011 Drill/Driver	6 V dc	8.8 V dc
Skil 2000 Cordless Screwdriver	5 V dc	5.16 V dc

The charging output cord can have a male or female plug (FIG. 6-7). This helps prevent the mistake of using an incorrect charger from a different unit, which can cause damage to the batteries. As plugs vary, so does the charging current.

Troubleshooting

Suspect a defective plug, cord, or charging circuit when improper voltage is measured at the output plug. Check to see if the charging cord might be broken where it enters the charging unit, or at the plug. The cord can break at either end with hard usage or if dropped and pulled on. To measure the voltage at the plug and transformer, insert two small pins through the center of each wire, at the body of the charger (FIG. 6-8). Plug the charger in and measure the voltage. Proceed to the male plug if voltage is measured; if not, suspect component breakdown inside the charger.

Replacing the plug

Replace the male plug if voltage is measured at the pins next to the male plug. Pull out the charger and cut off the defective plug or wire. Note that the wire with the white side tracer is the negative dc terminal. Usually the center terminal of the plug is positive, although many of the charging wires are not marked at all. Most of these plugs can be picked up at the electronic part stores. Make sure the dc polarity is correct before soldering up the male plug. Recheck the voltage and polarity after installing a new output plug.

Voltage measurement

When the charger indicates no output voltage, you can either repair it or purchase another one. Repairing the charger is not difficult; there are not many parts inside (FIG. 6-9).

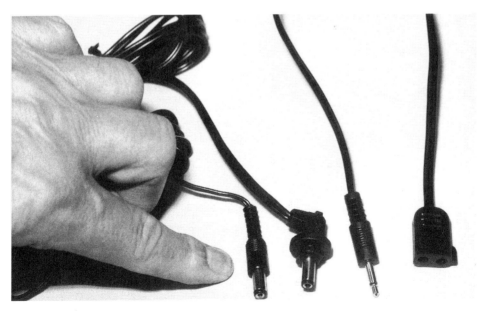

6-7 The different types of plugs found on the various chargers of small cordless power tools.

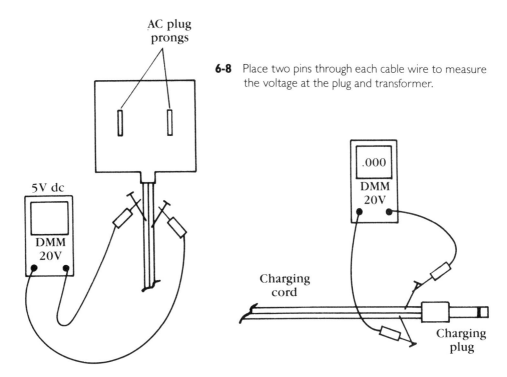

6-8 Place two pins through each cable wire to measure the voltage at the plug and transformer.

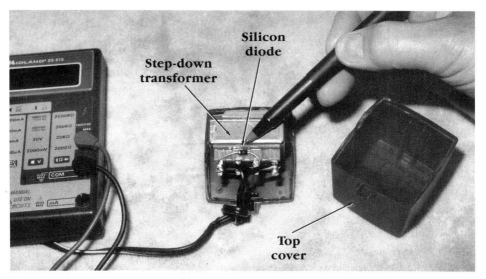

6-9 Only a few parts are found inside the battery charger of small cordless power tools.

First, take a resistance measurement across the ac plug of the charger. *Caution*: Do not take any resistance measurements with the charger plugged into the ac receptacle; unplug the unit. If the resistance measurements across the ac terminals are between 200 and 600 ohms, you may assume the ac wiring and transformer are good. No measurement might indicate that the winding of the transformer is open. If the transformer winding is open, purchase a new charger—it's not worth repairing.

Opening the unit

You might have noticed that these small chargers that plug directly into the outlet are similar to those found in the small portable radios or cordless razors. The unit is sealed at the bottom. Carefully take the hacksaw and cut above the sealed line of the charger body; be careful not to cut clean through. Do this to all four sides. Do not cut any cords, wires, or components while cutting or opening the plastic top area.

Thermal fuse

Some nickel-cadmium battery chargers have a thermal cutoff fuse embedded with the power transformer. These small thermal cutoff fuses have a metal body and ceramic ends with terminals soldered into the charging circuit. When the charging produces a certain amount of heat, the thermal fuse will open up contacts in the charging terminal lead. Charging of the battery will have to stop until after the thermal fuse has cooled down.

Repairing the charger

The charging circuit in small cordless tools is a simple rectifier dc circuit (FIG. 6-10). Only a few parts are located inside the charger. Check each diode using the digital multimeter. Replace the rectifier with a 1-amp silicon diode. Replace the filter capacitor if the voltage is lower than normal. Test the capacitor with a small capacitor tester. Check the continuity of the wiring with the low range of the ohmmeter. After making repairs and taking voltage output measurement, seal the cover with epoxy cement.

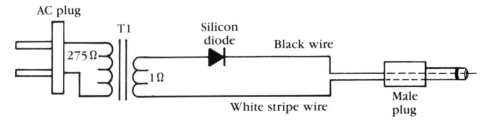

6-10   A typical charging circuit inside the charging unit of cordless power tools.

INSIDE THE CORDLESS TOOL

In the dc motor of the cordless power tool, the motor pulley drives the high-torque gearing assembly. A ball bearing thrust with sleeve bearings holds the chuck of the 3/8-inch drill (FIG. 6-11). Small ball bearings might be found at each end of the speed gears.

6-11 The gear train and ball bearings of the thrust and sleeve bearings.

The dc motor is powered by the small rechargeable nickel-cadmium power pack. The two-speed switch is mounted on the trigger lever to provide two different voltages to the dc motor. The forward/reverse switch on this model is mounted above the trigger assembly. In other models the switch might be mounted on the side or back of the tool. The forward position is used for drilling or driving screws, the reverse for backing out screws and jammed drill bits. The slower speed is used to replace or remove screws.

The batteries are located in the handle of the pistol grip area. The charging jack may be located at the back or end of the power drill. A convenient built-in chuck key holder or screwdriver tool might be clipped in the end of the handle for safekeeping.

Checking the motor

Check the voltage at the motor terminals with on/off switch on (FIG. 6-12). Suspect a weak battery if there is low or no voltage. Intermittent motor operation may be caused by a dirty or erratic switch, improper connections, or a defective motor. Clean up the switch terminals with cleaning fluid (FIG. 6-13). Make sure the motor terminals are soldered properly.

6-12   Check the voltage at the motor terminals with the switch on. Weak or no voltage may indicate a dirty switch or weak battery.

Check the motor using a different battery or voltage source, but that has the same voltage as the tool battery. Bypass all switches and use two clip leads from battery terminals to motor terminals. Now the motor is connected directly to the battery and should start to run. Monitor the battery terminals with the small voltmeter (FIG. 6-14). If the battery goes down very low, suspect a defective battery or shorted motor. Recharge the battery and make another test (TABLE 6-3).

SMALL SCREWDRIVER

The cordless screwdriver can have a straight body or one that bends in the middle. Usually, small screwdrivers are charged by a stationary charger mounted either vertically or horizontally. The screwdriver is clipped into the holder for charging or when not in use (FIG. 6-15). Make sure the screwdriver is pressed down to make good contact with the small battery charger.

6-13 Spray the switch terminals with cleaning fluid. Place the nozzle directly into the switch area.

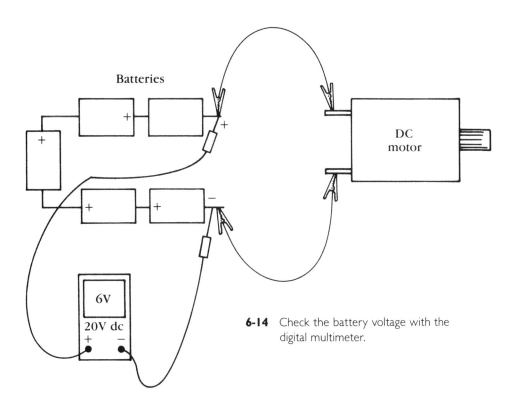

Batteries

DC motor

6V

20V dc

+   —

6-14 Check the battery voltage with the digital multimeter.

Table 6-3. Troubleshooting Chart for Cordless Power Tools

Problem	*Cause and Remedy*
Tool will not start	1. Charge the battery 2. Defective or dirty switch 3. Defective motor
Tool will not move reverse or forward	1. Check forward/reverse switch 2. Clean switch 3. Replace switch
Smoking motor	1. Check for inside arcing 2. Blow dust and dirt out of opening 3. Dry bearings 4. Overworked motor 5. Defective motor
Intermittent or erratic operation	1. Dirty on/off switch 2. Dirty speed switch 3. Broken switch assembly 4. Poor soldered connection 5. Defective motor
Noisy operation	1. Inspect gear train 2. Dry bearings or gears 3. Defective motor
Jammed tool	1. Check meshing of gears 2. Broken gears 3. Dry bearings and gears

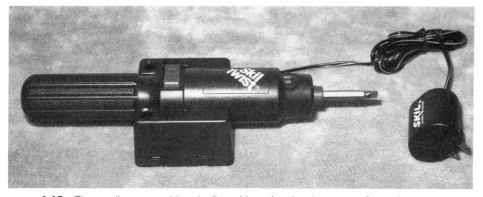

6-15   The cordless screwdriver is clipped into the charging mount for recharging.

The battery charger can be plugged into the power receptacle for any length of time. After the battery is charged, the cordless tool is ready to use; simply unclip it from the mounting stand. Do not operate the tool while in the charger. Notice the small charging stand has two small charging contacts that press tightly against the contact of the battery of screwdriver (FIG. 6-16). Keep these contacts clean by applying alcohol or cleaning fluid on a cotton stick.

6-16 Keep the charger contacts clean with cleaning fluid or alcohol.

Removing the covers

To remove the bottom cover of the small screwdriver, first remove the screws, then pry off the cover (FIG. 6-17). Make sure the top cover and tool is face down, so parts do not fall out. Remove the cover carefully to avoid damage.

Troubleshooting

Check the battery voltage if it will not charge up or seems weak (FIG. 6-18). Set the voltmeter to the 20-volt range. Inspect the on/off switch when the motor will not rotate. Clean up the off/on and reverse switch when the tool will not change direction. This switch might be one that you must hold down in order for the tool to operate in either direction. You can clip around any switch terminal with clip leads to determine if the switch is defective (FIG. 6-19).

Check the gear train for broken teeth or dry bearings. Apply a light coat of grease across the set of gears. Vaseline will work if you do not have any other light grease handy. If the motor runs but there is no movement of the drill chuck, or if there is a jammed chuck assembly, suspect broken teeth or gears. Some of the chuck assemblies can be rotated by hand to determine if the gear train is jammed.

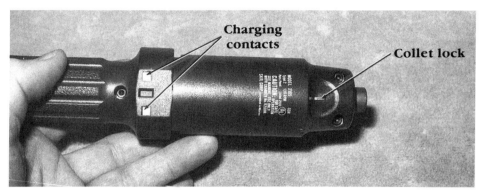

6-17 Remove body screws to gain access to the insides of the cordless screwdriver. Notice the location of the collet lock assembly.

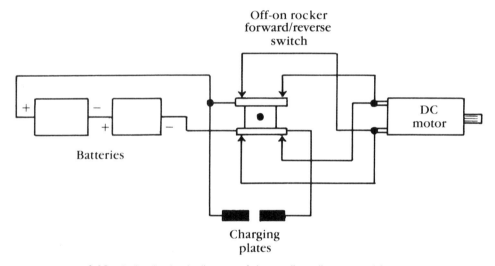

6-18 A simple circuit diagram of the small cordless screwdriver.

Replacing covers

Make sure all parts are in place. Double check the small bearings connected to the chuck shaft; these can slip to one side and not line up properly. Make sure the trigger and reverse switch are clicked in place. Push the batteries down tightly. Check all small wiring so it will not be pinched when the top cover is replaced.

Firmly fit the cover over all parts. The chuck assembly might have to be held into position to get the cover on. Clip the two plastic sides together and replace all cover screws. Remember, some of the body screws might be a different length than those used in the handle of the power tool. Slightly tighten one screw at the chuck, top end, and bottom end of plastic cover so that all sides are bolted together. Now completely tighten up each screw.

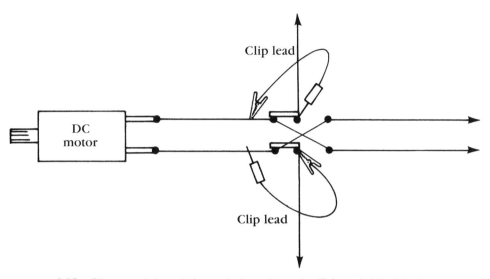

6-19 Clip around the switch terminals to determine if the switch is defective.

The collet lock

Most small cordless screwdrivers are equipped with a collet lock. This will lock the collet in one position while you tighten or loosen a nut or screw by rotating the screwdriver by hand. This is done with the switch off; do not turn on the forward or reverse button while the collet lock is on. Also, the collet lock is handy when the battery is low and does not have enough power to complete the job. Make sure the lock is off when operating the power tool.

Push down the collet lock to engage it (FIG. 6-20). Make sure the top side of the tool is facing upward. If the collet lock will not engage, place the bit into a screw and rotate the screwdriver by hand in either direction, while pushing down upon collet lock. Push the collet lock up to disengage the lock. Make sure the lock is not on while operating the tool.

6-20 Push lever down to engage the collet lock.

PISTOL GRIP REVERSIBLE SCREWDRIVER

This type of cordless screwdriver has more power than the small straight screwdriver, which means you can exert more pressure, especially when removing screws. The model shown here operates with three batteries at 3.9 volts. The plug-in charger has a 5-volt dc charging rate (FIG. 6-21). Notice the different type charging plug. The white trace wire is the negative terminal.

6-21 The small charger has a 5-volt dc charging rate with load attached. Notice the negative white tracer wire in the cord.

Removing the cover

When taking off the cover of the screwdriver, first remove the four body screws (FIG. 6-22). Use the correct tool to remove these small screws. Carefully pry off the top plastic cover. A thin pocketknife blade may be inserted around the bottom pistol edge to pop off the cover. Be careful when removing the cover; the spring-loaded trigger switch can cause the trigger assembly to fall out of place (FIG. 6-23).

Replacing the batteries

Remove the motor and gear assembly by unclipping the wires to the motor. A white wire runs to the bottom side and the red wire runs from the switch to the top motor terminal. The motor and gear assembly can be removed from the gun assembly. Remove three small screws to separate the motor from the gear assembly (FIG. 6-24).

6-22 Remove these four screws to remove the top plastic piece. Keep power tool flat when removing covers.

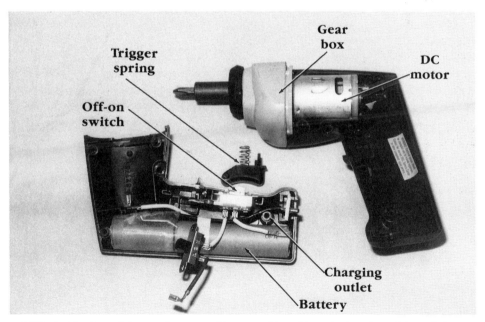

6-23 Inside view of the cordless reversible screwdriver. Note the location of the switches.

The simple wiring circuit includes the batteries, motor, momentary on switch and forward/reverse switch, and protection diode (FIG. 6-25). The protection diode is inserted in the lead of battery. You must hold the pistol trigger switch to conclude the series circuit. Remove the batteries by unclipping the end terminals.

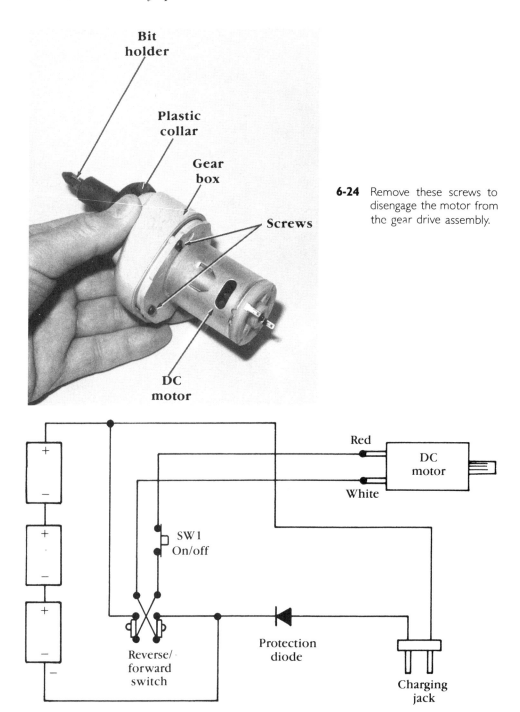

6-24 Remove these screws to disengage the motor from the gear drive assembly.

6-25 The simplified wiring circuit of the cordless screwdriver.

Notice only two battery sections are shown, although three batteries are found in the battery container (FIG. 6-26). Remove the tape holding the connecting wires to the battery body. Replace the batteries, making sure to use the correct polarity.

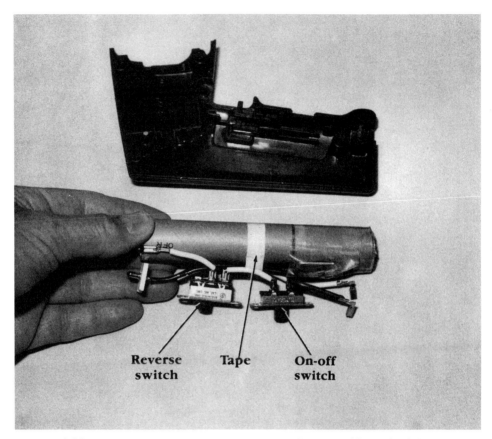

Reverse   **Tape**   **On-off**
switch   **switch**

6-26 Remove tape from body of batteries to disengage wiring and switches.

Troubleshooting

Suspect poor connections and dirty switches if there is a problem with erratic operation. Clean up each switch with cleaning spray. Measure the continuity of the motor with the low-ohm range of the ohmmeter. Often, worn out brushes can cause the motor circuit to open. Replace the motor only if the replacement does not exceed the cost of a new tool.

When the battery will not charge, suspect a defective battery, charger, or silicon diode. Check the diode using the digital multimeter. Now reverse the leads. A good silicon diode will show a measurement in only one direction (FIG. 6-27). No reading in either direction indicates that the transistor is open; a reading in both directions indicates a shorted diode.

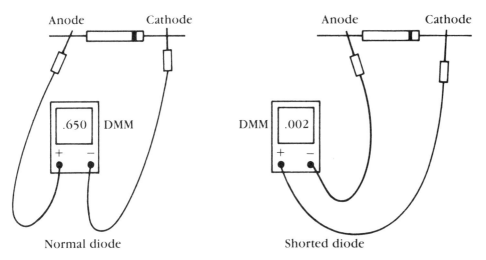

6-27 A normal protection diode test measures in one direction, while a shorted diode indicates a low ohm measurement in both directions.

THE ³/₈-INCH HAND DRILL

The ³/₈-inch cordless drill operates at two speeds: 200 and 500 RPM (FIG. 6-28). To operate at slow speed, or 200 RPM, squeeze the trigger switch halfway. Squeeze the switch all the way to 500 RPM for normal drilling operations. A control or reversing switch changes the polarity of the battery voltage at the motor terminals, which also allows the tool to operate in both forward and reverse directions.

6-28 This ³/₈-inch cordless drill has forward and reverse speeds, as well as low (200 RPM) and high (500 RPM) speeds.

Troubleshooting

When the drill will not change speeds, suspect a dirty high/low switch. If the drill will not reverse, suspect a dirty or broken forward/reverse switch. First try cleaning the switches. Then check continuity of switch terminals with ohmmeter. Replace the switch if it cannot be cleaned.

A protection diode is found between the positive terminal of the battery and charging jack. Check if the diode is open condition when the charger will not charge up the batteries (FIG. 6-29). Inspect the connections and dirty elements of the charging jack outlet. Clean up the jack with cleaning fluid or alcohol. Notice if the charging becomes intermittent if the charging plug is rotated in the jack.

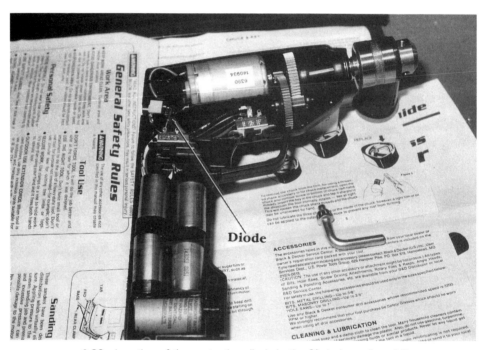

6-29 Location of the protection diode in the ³/₈-inch cordless drill.

Inspect the chuck and gear assembly for broken teeth or dry bearings. Here the large chuck and drive gear have self lubricating ball bearings (FIG. 6-30), so periodic relubricating might not be required. Of course, if the bearings do become dry or noisy, a squirt of light oil or grease upon the gears can solve the problem.

The drill chuck may be removed by removing a small screw inside the chuck jaws. Spray a light silicone oil cleaning spray inside the chuck area if the jaws are difficult to close or open. Make sure the sleeve bearings are in the groove before replacing the chuck gear assembly.

6-30 Inspect the chuck and gear assembly for broken teeth or dry bearings.

Voltage measurement

Measure the voltage of the batteries after the charger has been attached for 3 to 5 hours. The fully charged battery should measure about 6 volts. When replacing batteries, unclip the connections. Mark where each wire is located for easy replacement (FIG. 6-31). Remember, in a two-speed cordless drill or driver, one of the batteries is tapped, so three different terminals must be removed from the battery pack.

TWO-SPEED REVERSING DRILL AND DRIVER

The cordless reversing drill and driver is designed to drill holes and drive screws using two different speeds. This cordless tool has a 600 RPM speed for drilling and 400 RPM for driving screws (FIG. 6-32).

The chuck key is clipped in place at the top of the drill and the driver blade is located in the slot at the bottom of the handle.

The charging outlet is in the back side of the handle. A trigger, lock, and reversing switch is found above the trigger assembly, while the high and low speed switch is located opposite the chuck in the drill body (FIG. 6-33). Change drill direction only when chuck is completely stopped.

To remove the bottom cover, take out the screws and carefully pry up both ends of the plastic cover (FIG. 6-34). Notice the battery arrangement and wiring. Four small batteries are used for the high speed, three for the low speed (FIG. 6-35).

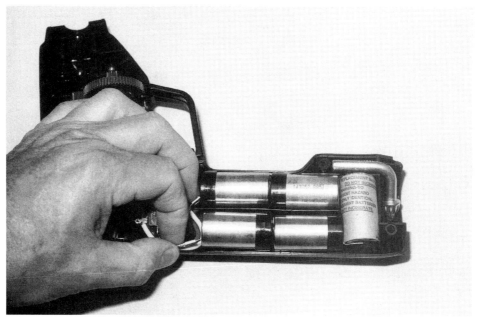

6-31   Before removing the batteries in this drill, mark down all three terminals. The center volt-age top runs to the two-speed switch.

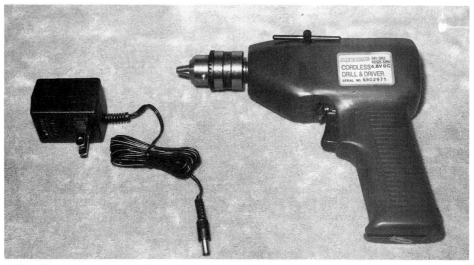

6-32   The two-speed reversible drill operates at 400 RPM for driving and 600 RPM for drilling.

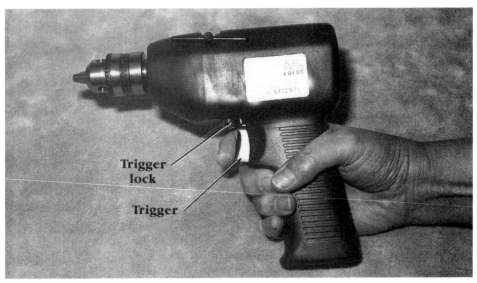

6-33   The trigger, lock, and reversing switch are located on trigger assembly. The speed switch is located at the back of the drill.

6-34   Remove the body screws to take off the bottom plastic cover.

6-35 Carefully pry up the cover from both ends.

TWO-SPEED DRILL KIT

The Dremel cordless power tool can be a high-speed grinder, carver, polisher, sander, cutter, brush, and drill. The tool includes all of these attachments (FIG. 6-36).

The tool can run at both high and low speeds. The low speed is best for polishing operations, and for delicate wood carving and cutting out small model parts. The high speed is best for carving, cutting, routing, shaping, and jointing.

Removing the cover

To remove the bottom cover, take off the body screws and unscrew the plastic collar at the chuck (FIG. 6-37). All components can be removed separately. The front gear and keyless chuck pull out from the motor shaft (FIG. 6-38). Now the motor can be unclipped from the circuit.

Changing collets

A collet lock is located at the bottom and front shaft assembly. Four different size collets are available with this power tool. The shaft collet must be locked into position when changing different collets. Do not operate the motor while the power tool is running or while collet is locked in.

6-36 The cordless two-speed Dremel drill kit.

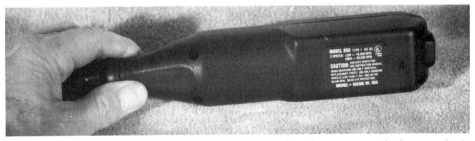

6-37 Remove the body screws and the plastic front cover in order to remove the bottom plastic cover.

To install a different collet, remove the collet nut, then the old collet. Insert the slotted end of the new collet into the hole in the end of the tool shaft. Replace collet nut on the shaft. Always use the collet that matches the shank size of the accessory you plan to use. Be careful not to force a larger diameter shaft into a small collet.

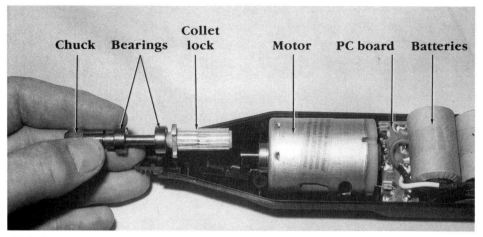

6-38 The front collet chuck assembly may be pulled off of the plastic connection that fits over the motor shaft.

Charging

For light-duty work, this small power tool can be operated for about 35 continuous minutes before the batteries must be recharged. For medium work, such as drilling soft wood, figure 10 to 12 minutes. To grind, sand, or polish metal the tool may operate continuously for 25 to 30 minutes. For heavy-duty work the cordless tool will operate only 8 to 10 minutes.

Although this small tool operates from the 6-volt battery, the charger is a 7.5-volt ac transformer. While most chargers produce a dc voltage to charge the cordless tool batteries, this power tool has a silicon diode mounted on the switchboard. Also, a small LED will light when the charger supplies ac voltage to the power tool circuits (FIG. 6-39). The batteries may be unclipped for easy replacement.

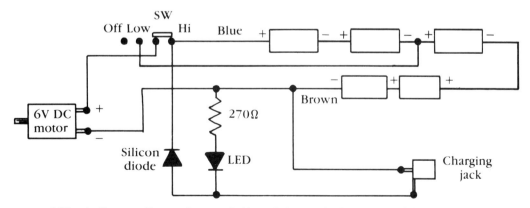

6-39 A silicon rectifier on the pc switchboard charges the five nickel-cadmium batteries.

When the tool will not operate on slow speed and turns slowly on high speed, suspect a weak battery. Charge up the battery for 3 hours. If the problem continues, check the charge voltage at the positive terminal of the silicon diode and brown wire. Does the charging light come on? Replace the small dc motor if there is no rotation of the motor after applying 6 volts to the motor terminals (FIG. 6-40).

6-40 The charger plugs directly into the ac receptacle and furnishes 7.5 volts ac to the charger outlet jack, instead of a dc voltage like other cordless drills.

Check the ac charging voltage at the charging plug. Suspect a broken wire or dirty jack if there is no voltage. If the light is on and there is low or no charging voltage at the batteries, test for an open or shorted silicon diode. If the charging light is out and battery charges anyway, suspect a broken voltage dropping resistor or LED.

Replacing motor unit

Be careful when replacing the motor unit into the plastic cover. Often, the small spring on the collet lock will come off when the motor and shaft assembly is removed (FIG. 6-41). The small tension spring feeds through the plastic lock switch to a round plastic post. Clip the circle end of the spring over the plastic post with a pair of long-nose pliers. The bottom cover will hold the switch lever to lock the collet into place. Make sure the plastic lever works freely and snaps into place after the back is on. Double check that the small charging jack fits into the plastic indentations; if not, the cover will not go on.

GRASS TRIMMER

The cordless grass trimmer makes lawn care easier. It does not require gasoline or an electric cord (FIG. 6-42). Before using the tool the first time allow it to charge up for about 16 hours. The trimmer will operate for about 30 minutes before it needs another charge. After this initial use, the batteries will charge back up to full capacity in about 2 hours.

Charging

To recharge, the cordless trimmer is placed in a wall-mounted charging base (FIG. 6-43). The batteries should be charged at around 75° Fahrenheit. While charging, the charger will become warm to the touch.

If you notice that operating time is reduced, it could be that the battery was only partially discharged when you attempted to recharge it. Run the trimmer until it stops, then charge the battery again for 16 hours. This procedure might have to be repeated a few times for best results.

A lock off button is located at the top of the trimmer and will prevent the trigger switch from being turned on. This prevents accidental operation when dismounting the tool or while handling the cordless shears (FIG. 6-44).

Trimmer maintenance

Use mild soap and a damp cloth to clean up the cordless trimmer. Dry off and spray the blades with a can of lubricant. This should be done after each cleanup. Do not use gasoline, turpentine, or paint thinner around the plastic body. Keep the housing out of the rain and do not submerge in water. Always run the trimmer for a few minutes first to clean off all excess grass and debris.

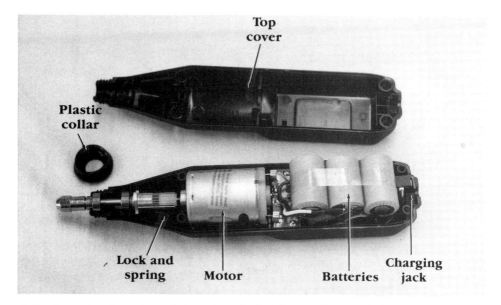

6-41 A small tension spring pulls back the collet lock button. Be careful it does not fall out when removing the motor or shaft.

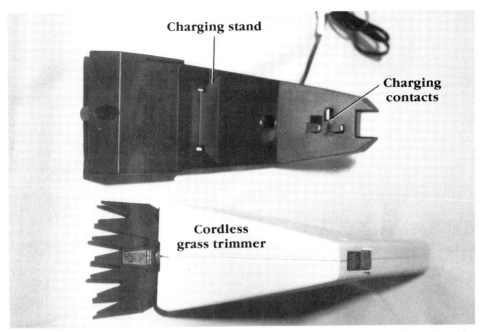

Charging stand

Charging contacts

Cordless grass trimmer

6-42 The cordless grass and weed trimmer is handy for touching up lawn or garden edging. You do not need gasoline or an electric cord.

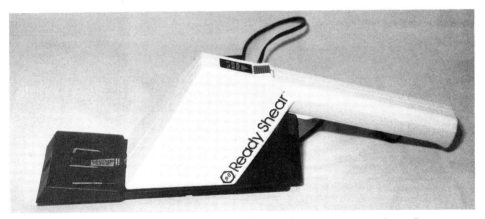

6-43 The cordless trimmer is placed in the charging mount on the wall.

If the cordless trimmer is dropped accidentally, check the blades for bent areas. If blades are bent out of shape, they should be replaced. Check the housing for cracked or broken areas. Make sure the lock off switch works. Nicked blades may be used only if it does not prevent the meshing of the teeth.

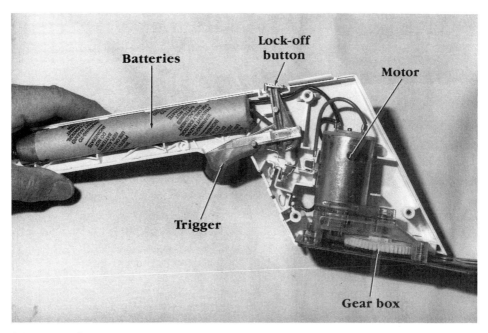

6-44 A lock/off button prevents the trimmer from turning on accidentally while handling or removing the tool from the charging mount.

6-45 Remove three screws to take off the cutting blades from the bottom of the trimmer.

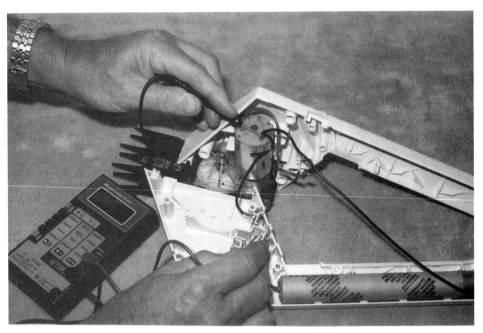

6-46   The nickel-cadmium batteries are located inside a long tube.

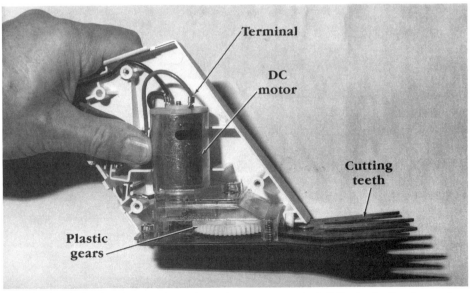

6-47   Check the dc voltage on batteries and at motor terminals if the tool will not operate.

Replace the blades after one year of heavy use. Sharpen blades if they become dull. To remove the blades, simply take out the three screws in the bottom of the tool, and the blades are free (FIG. 6-45). These blades may be removed and cleaned. Be sure and line up the small gear and washer with the slotted area of the blade. The top set of teeth are stationary, while the bottom blade moves back and forwards to cut the grass or weeds.

Charge the batteries when the unit slows down (FIG. 6-46). If the batteries will not charge, check the dc voltage of the charger. Check the dc voltage across the motor if the motor will not rotate (FIG. 6-47). If the blades move slowly, suspect gummed or dry gears. Check the on/off switch if the tool does not operate. Remove the blade assembly when working on the tool.

Chapter **7**

Nine small power tools

$\mathcal{S}$mall power tools—drill, sander, jig and saber saw, bench grinder, power stapler, electric glue gun, pencil engraver, and electric weed trimmer—are common in many workshops, and carry much of the work-load for home repairs and projects. Keeping these tools in good shape with proper care and maintenance takes very little time or effort.

SAFETY

Safety rules should be followed with any power tool; there are a few added safety features for small hand tools:

- Keep bits and blades sharp for making clean holes and cuts. Do not use drilling tools to burn or rip holes in wood.
- Always unplug the drill when attaching another bit. Remove the key before starting up the drill.
- Don't force the tool. It will do a better and safer job at the rate for which it was designed.
- Do not overwork tool to the point that it starts to smoke; you can quickly burn up the motor windings.
- Choose the right tool for the right job. The small hand drill should not be used for big jobs.
- Secure the work with clamps or a vise when drilling, sawing, or cutting. This leaves both hands free to run the small power tool.
- Store tools in a dry place, and lock them in a cabinet to avoid danger to children.
- Wipe off tools after each job. Clean off plastic body with soap and water. Wipe light oil on the metal parts to prevents rust and keep a shiny surface.

- Inspect all cords and plugs for tears, breaks, and loose connections. Do not pull on the cord when removing the plug from the socket.
- Do not remove the ground plug from the small power tool to make it fit into the extension cord or ungrounded receptacle. Purchase the necessary three-prong attachment.

HAND DRILL

The small hand drill may be the most overworked of any tool (FIG. 7-1). It is used mostly to drill holes up to ⅜ inch in diameter, but also has attachments for polishing, sanding, and grinding.

7-1 The small electric hand drill can be used for drilling, polishing, sanding, and grinding operations.

Inside the hand drill

The electric drill consists of a small ac motor with armature and brushes. The motor drives a set of reduction gears to the motor shaft. An adjustable chuck is attached to the end of the shaft to accept the different size bits. The electric motor is turned on by a switch, usually a trigger type.

Troubleshooting

Many drill problems are related to a defective power cord. Often the cord is yanked rather than pulled, from the outlet which can damage the cord and plug. If the motor will not rotate, inspect the plug and cord for broken or loose wires. Use the ohmmeter to take a continuity reading across the male plug terminals (FIG. 7-2). This measurement should be under 15 ohms. If the drill runs intermittently, it might have a high reading. Suspect poor brushes, a broken cord, or a defective switch.

7-2   Measure the resistance across the male plug prongs with switch on to check for an open motor, broken cord, or bad switch.

If too much pressure is exerted on the drill while operating, it can run hot and damage the motor and bearings. If the motor is run for an extended period of time, it is possible to burn up the motor armature. Avoid overworking the drill. Feel the body of the motor: If it is too warm to touch, let it cool down before further use.

To check for a defective switch, clip the ohmmeter leads across the switch and take a continuity reading (FIG. 7-3). Pull the trigger off and on. If the trigger is lifeless, suspect a broken switch. If the ohmmeter measurement is shorted and the meter is open the next time it is clicked, suspect a dirty or intermittent switch. If the resistance measurement is over 1 ohm, suspect burned switch contacts. First, clean up the switch with cleaning fluid. Replace the switch if problems continue.

7-3 Clip the ohmmeter across the switch to determine if it is open or dirty.

Inspecting the brushes

Examine the brushes by removing the back or side body (FIG. 7-4). Replace the brushes if they are excessively worn or if arcing at the brushes and armature indicates poor brush contact. These motor brushes can be picked up at the manufacturer's service center or local motor repair shop.

Remove body screws to get at the brushes and motor assembly (FIG. 7-5). In some hand drills, you will need to remove the back handle assembly. If the motor hums but does not run, suspect a jammed gear assembly or frozen bearings. Suspect damaged gears when the chuck moves slowly and is very noisy (FIG. 7-6). A dry bearing might also be noisy and begin to squeal. Lubricate the motor bearings with Number 10 or 20 motor oil. Wash out the bearings with cleaning fluid first if grease is caked on. Too much oil can short out the field and cause the armature to arc.

Inspecting the gear assembly

To inspect the gear assembly for worn gears or a dry gear box, remove the four screws in the front plate of the drill (FIG. 7-7). Then remove the front end cap with a sleeve bearing. Inspect the gear assembly for caked grease, which can cause the drill to slow down. Wash out the old grease and apply a light grease over the gear teeth. Most gear case assemblies have been completely lubricated at the factory and should not need to be touched for at least a year, under normal operation.

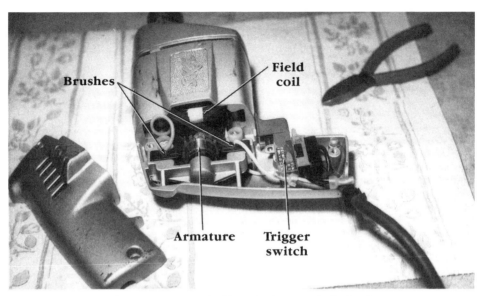

7-4 Remove the back side or body to reach the brushes.

7-5 Remove external screws to get at the motor assembly.

Remove the brushes with a flat screwdriver (FIG. 7-8). Often the back cover must be removed to gain access to the brushes. Replace the brushes if they are worn. Inspect the wire clip that connects the brush assembly to the circuit. Use the ohmmeter to check the field windings for an open coil or bad connections (FIG. 7-9). Remove the armature and inspect the soldered connections on the copper commutator.

7-6   Wash out bearings if caked with dirt and grime, and lubricate with light oil.

7-7   Inspect the gear assembly for worn gears or a dry gear box.

THE ¹/₄ HORSEPOWER VARIABLE SPEED DRILL

This variable speed reversing ³/₈-inch power drill is compact, light in weight, balanced, and easy to use (FIG. 7-10). The drill has the following attachments: drill, hole saw, wire brush, buffer, polishing pad, sanding disc, and grinding wheel. The speed is controlled by the trigger switch, which also allows the tool to operate both forward and reverse.

Inside the drill

For inspection or repair, remove the cover by unscrewing the body screws (FIG. 7-11). Notice that the drill has air-cooled, ball-thrust, and permanently lubricated sleeve bearings for longer life. The double gear reduction system provides high power. Notice also that the brushes are enclosed in the three-position switch assembly (FIG. 7-12). At the bottom of the speed switch is a lock that will allow the drill to run at full speed.

Troubleshooting

The total motor, brush, and armature resistance that feeds the variable speed switch is 12 ohms. When taking a resistance measurement, if the resistance from motor is somewhere around 8 to 20 ohms, you may assume the motor is normal.

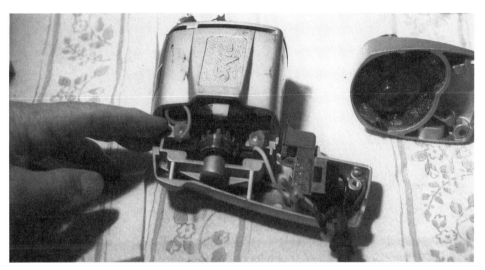

7-8 Use a screwdriver to remove the brushes. Note the plastic brush holders.

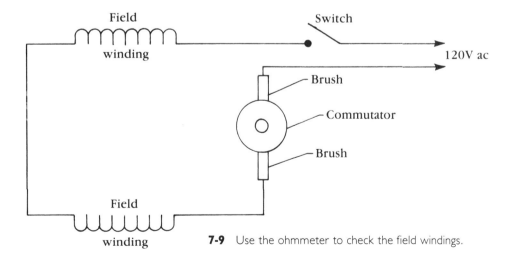

7-9 Use the ohmmeter to check the field windings.

7-10   The 1/4 horsepower variable speed drill is small and easy to handle.

7-11   Remove external screws to take off the top cover.

Although some of the variable speed reversing drills have an induction motor, this drill still has the series wound circuit with brushes and armature. If the drill runs erratically, try cleaning the contacts in the three-position switch. Work the switch back and forth after spraying cleaning fluid down in the plastic switch contact area. Avoid getting fluid on the brushes and commutator (FIG. 7-13).

7-12 The brushes are enclosed in the reversible switch assembly.

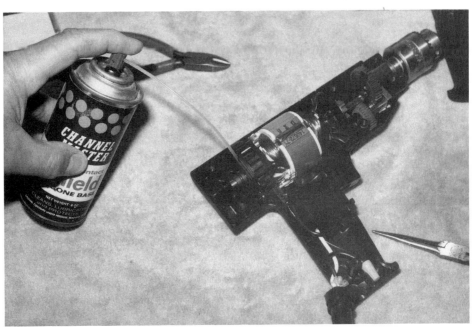

7-13 Clean off the switch assembly contacts when motor runs erratically. Spray cleaning fluid down into switch area. Be careful not to get fluid on brushes and commutator.

Excessive noise from the gear box assembly might be cured with an application of light oil on the gears and shaft. The chuck can be removed by opening the chuck jaws and removing the small screw. Be careful not to loosen the small thrust ball bearing at the end of the chuck assembly.

Clean off the plastic case of the drill with a damp cloth and household cleaning agent. Do not use solvents such as gasoline, turpentine, or paint thinner on the plastic case.

PALM SANDER

The palm or finishing sander is ideal for finishing wood projects. This electric sander is easy to operate, and much faster than hand sanding (FIG. 7-14). Always operate the sander with the wood grain. Clean the sander after each job. Brush or blow out the fine dust from the brush air openings. Excessive firing might result when dust collects on the armature commutator surface.

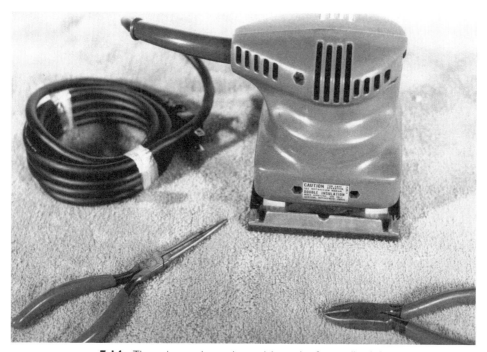

7-14 The palm sander makes quick work of a sanding job.

Safety

In addition to general electric power tool safety rules, check those listed by the manufacturer. Here are some helpful rules to follow when using the small electric sander:

- Be careful to maintain proper paper tension.
- Align the edges of the sanding paper with either edge of the pad. Do not use sanding paper that is larger than the pad of the palm sander.
- Replace the sanding paper if worn or torn in areas.
- Operate the sander with the wood grain to prevent sanding marks on the finished area.
- Make sure the teeth of the clamper grips the sand paper. If the paper becomes loose or slips, it could result in uneven sanding.
- Remove only a small amount of material at a time. Do not bear down on the sander; heavy pressure could damage sanding paper and the tool.
- Never run the tool without proper abrasive paper; the pad is easily damaged.
- Clean up, brush off, and wipe off the small sander after each sanding job. Wipe light motor oil upon metal surfaces to prevent rust forming, especially when not using the tool for long periods.
- Do not forget to send in the warranty registration after purchasing the new sander.

Inside the sander

With this particular sander, the on/off switch is at the top front for easy operation. Simply slide the switch back and forth to start and stop the sanding operation.

To open the tool for repair on inspection, simply remove both plastic side panels by taking off the four bolts and nuts. Remove the cast aluminum felt pad assembly by unscrewing the shaft and flywheel (FIG. 7-15).

Troubleshooting

Suspect a broken cord, ac plug, or defective switch when the motor will not operate. Measure the continuity of the motor, cord, and brushes by clipping the ohmmeter across the ac plug. Unplug the sander when taking this measurement. The resistance should be 20 to 30 ohms (FIG. 7-16). If the resistance measurement is quite high, suspect a dirty switch or improperly seated brushes.

Replace the entire cord and plug if the cord is accidentally cut or becomes frayed and worn. Feed the cord through the cord guard and solder to the respective connections. Notice this small sander does not have a three-prong ground plug, because the body of the sander has double insulated plastic housing.

After the sides are removed, check the brushes for proper seating (FIG. 7-17). Clean off the commutator with cleaning fluid or alcohol. Replace the brush and spring if ground down and will not seat properly. Use the ohmmeter to check the continuity of the armature wires feeding each capper section. The readings should be about the same. Likewise, check the continuity of the field coils.

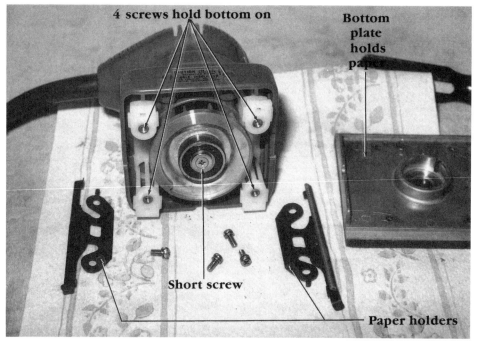

4 screws hold bottom on

Bottom plate holds paper

Short screw

Paper holders

7-15 Remove the felt pad assembly. Here, the shaft screw and flywheel must be removed before the sides can be taken off.

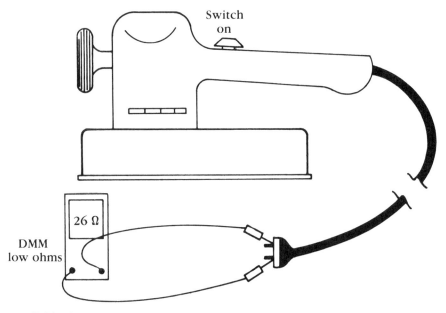

Switch on

26 Ω

DMM low ohms

7-16 Check resistance across the ac plug for an open cord, switch, or motor.

7-17   Inspect the brushes for proper seating. Replace if completely worn down.

Inspect the ball bearings at each end of the motor shaft. Notice if dust has collected in the ball bearing areas (FIG. 7-18). Clean with cleaning spray and lubricate with a light motor oil. Do not allow oil to drip on the commutator and brushes. The disassembled palm sander is shown in FIG. 7-19.

ORBITAL FINISHING SANDER

The orbital finish sander (FIG. 7-20) has dual action: it sands in a straight line or orbitally. The orbital action is for fast removal of material and the straight sanding action is for a finer, swirl-free finish. The plastic handle permits better control for uniform sanding.

Most finishing sanders have permanently lubricated bronze bearings. However, if a bearing becomes noisy and makes a screeching sound, lubricate bearings with light motor oil. First, clean or wash out all dust particles from inside the motor housing.

Troubleshooting

To take off the plastic body for inspection or repair, remove the screws, then lift it off (FIG. 7-21). An operating switch is found at the top of the large grip handle.

7-18 Inspect the ball bearings at each end of the motor shaft.

Check the seating of brushes. If you need access to the brush and spring assembly, first remove the two small plastic covers. Inspect the armature commutator for normal soldered connections (FIG. 7-22).

If the problem is erratic or intermittent operation, check the switch. Clean it out with cleaning fluid, spraying fluid right down into the switch contacts. Work the switch back and forth. Now check the resistance of the switch with the ohmmeter (FIG. 7-23). A dead short should be found across the switch terminals. Make sure the tool is not plugged in. Erratic or low ohms of resistance might indicate dirty or burned switch contacts. Replace it with original part number. When measured across the ac plug, the total resistance of the orbital sander should be around 22 ohms.

Inspect the pad assembly if the sander will not reverse from straight to orbital sanding. Remove the screws and drop down the pad assembly. Check the ball bearing and plastic housing (FIG. 7-24). Look for broken teeth or a worn gear box.

7-19 Layout of the palm sander.

7-20 The orbital finishing sander.

7-21 Remove external screws to lift off the plastic body of the small sander.

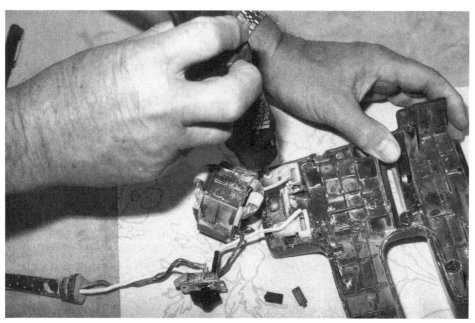

7-22 Remove small covers to reach the brush assemblies.

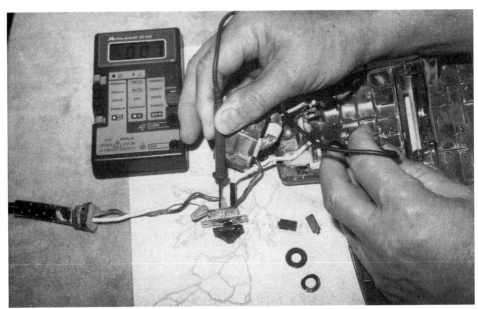

7-23 Check the switch contacts with the ohmmeter. A low resistance measurement indicates dirty or burned contacts.

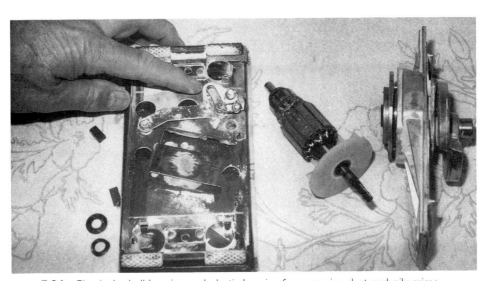

7-24 Check the ball bearing and plastic housing for excessive dust and oily grime.

Excessive noise in the motor assembly might be caused by dry or worn bearings, worn gears, or a metal fan blade (FIG. 7-25). Check the bronze bearings of the gear assembly and motor. Suspect jammed helical gear assembly when the motor hums without rotation.

7-25 Dry bearings or worn gears can cause noise during operation.

JIG OR SABER SAW

After the small drill, the small jig or saber saw is probably the most popular and most heavily used tool. They are handy for so many different jobs. The jigsaw can cut hard or soft wood, metal, composition board, or plastic by simply changing the blade. Jig or saber saws can have fixed or variable speeds (FIG. 7-26).

7-26 The saber saw.

Fastening the blade

Make sure the saw blade is securely fastened in place. Most jigsaws have a small bolt that tightens down on the edge of the saw blade. Push the blade completely in before tightening the small screw head. Use the correct screwdriver to avoid damaging the screw head.

Troubleshooting

Broken cords, plugs, or switches cause most of the problems in these saws (FIG. 7-27). Replace the entire cord if it becomes ragged or cut. If the tool is operating intermittently, try cleaning the on/off switch with cleaning spray. Inspect the variable speed switch and wire contacts when the jigsaw will not change speeds. Brush and wash out all dust and dirt that has accumulated inside the motor housing.

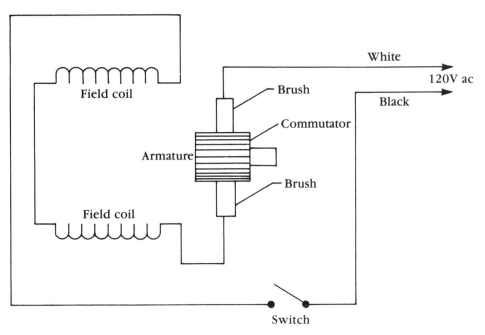

7-27 Check the jig or saber saw for broken cords, plugs, and switches.

Excessive arcing of brushes might be caused by defective brushes or dust accumulation on the armature. Suspect a jammed or dry gear box when the motor hums but the drill will not operate. Overheating of the motor and damage to the gear assembly can occur when using dull blades, because excess pressure is applied to force the cutting of the wood. Avoid this by replacing worn blades.

Remove the body screws of the saber saw to reach the brushes. Inspect the brushes for worn grooves in the armature. Remove each brush to determine if any need to be replaced. Check the rear motor bearing for worn or dry bearings (FIG. 7-28).

7-28 Check the rear motor bearing for wear or dry bearings.

The front cover can be removed to inspect the reciprocating shaft and gears. Clean out old grease and caked dust (FIG. 7-29). Get down inside the housing area with a small brush. Lubricate the sliding shaft with light motor oil or grease. Remove the brushes before pulling the armature assembly from the back housing (FIG. 7-30). Wipe off the armature before replacing.

Remove the two screws holding the shaft assembly to the motor housing (FIG. 7-31), then remove the large shaft. Clean it with cleaning fluid. Clean the gear box of caked grease and dust particles. Repack gear box with a light grease and apply light oil to the reciprocating shaft. Check the fan blade for loose mounting, which can produce a scraping noise. Reassemble the saw.

BENCH SANDER

The small bench sander with a wide belt is ideal for sanding flat and end pieces of wood. This unique 4-inch belt sander has a self-contained motor (FIG. 7-32). There are no drive belts or pulleys to purchase or adjust. The motor speed is adjusted with the electronic speed control. The belt sander can be used to finish wood, non-ferrous metal, or plastic—with the proper belt and belt speed.

7-29 Clean the grease and sawdust from the gear and reciprocating slide bar.

7-30 Remove the brushes before pulling the armature from the motor assembly.

7-31   Remove the two screws holding the shaft assembly to the motor housing.

7-32   Front view of the 4-inch belt sander.

Safety

In addition to the general safety rules for all electric tools, also consider these safety measures that are particular to the small bench sander:

- Make sure all parts are attached—especially the tilt table—before operating the power sander.
- Keep hands and fingers away from the belt when adjusting the speed control or when turning the sander on.
- Make adjustments with the power off. Make tracking adjustments with the power on at low speeds.
- Adjust the tilt table wear plate within $\frac{1}{14}$ inch of the belt to avoid pinching the workpiece or fingers between the table and belt.
- Make sure all adjustable parts are tight and secure so they cannot loosen up while sanding.
- Install the proper belt for the job: follow the guide directions.
- Trim all frayed belt ends.
- Exert moderate pressure against the sanding belt; do not press hard. Hold work firmly against the table.
- Make sure the belt sander is mounted permanently before operating.
- Do not wet the sanding belt or allow water to enter the tool. Prevent electrical shock hazards.
- Keep an open flame or heat source away from the plastic sander housing.
- Operate sander in well-ventilated areas.
- Do not sand magnesium, asbestos, paint, or other materials that could create flammable or injurious dust.
- When servicing, use identical replacement parts.
- Keep the power cord away from the sanding belt.
- Always wear goggles to protect your eyes.

Adjustments

The on/off switch, safety key, variable speed control, and belt tracking knob are found on the front cover housing. The deflector fence, deflector fence knob, wear plate adjustment screw, aluminum table, drive roller, tilt table wear plate, table tilting knob, and meter gauge slot are found in the belt path. The belt tensioning lever, vacuum cleaning port, rear tension roller, front end roller, drive belt housing, and cord storage area are located at the opposite or rear side. (FIG. 7-33).

Follow the manufacturer's literature for mounting and adjusting the meter gauge, deflector fence, and tilting sander table. Know how to set the safety key off/on switch, variable speed control, and belt tensioning for correct operation before attempting to use the small bench sander.

7-33   Rear side view of the belt sander.

Changing the sanding belt

Correct installation of a new sanding belt is very important. If the belt isn't properly adjusted, the edges can become worn and tear, snag on material, and slip off. All belt should be centered over rollers while in operation. Follow these steps when changing the belt:

- Switch the off/on button to the off position.
- Remove the safety key.
- Unplug the sander from the ac receptacle.
- Remove the deflector fence.
- Release any belt tension levers; they should be in the unlocked position.
- Grasp the belt at the tension roller and pull it off towards you. The belt should release. Pull with equal pressure at both ends so the belt will not bind.
- Install the belt over the rollers, being careful not to kink or bind the belt. Make sure the belt arrow is pointing in the direction that the sander rotates.
- Turn the sander on. Adjust tension levers so the belt rides in the center of all rollers. Recheck the position of the new belt after a few minutes of operation. Keep speed low until the belt is properly centered.

Troubleshooting

When making inspections or repairs, take off the front plastic cover by removing the screws (FIG. 7-34). Brush and clean out all grinding dust and particles from the sander. Tip the unit to one side to release excess accumulation, if it is not bolted down. Inspect the rollers for binding. The belt should be removed so you can check each roller. A vacuum cleaner nozzle fits in the main housing at the back side of this bench sander.

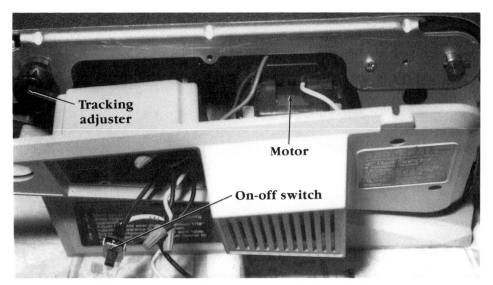

7-34 Remove external screws to remove the front plastic cover.

If the motor won't start, check the safety key position and the on/off switch. Make sure the tool is plugged into the receptacle. Double check the speed control setting; if it is set to a low speed it occasionally will not start up. Remove the ac plug and inspect the cord for possible breaks or cut areas.

Use the ohmmeter to check the ac plug for continuity (FIG. 7-35). If there is no measurement, suspect a defective switch or worn brushes. Inspect the on/off switch for possible open contacts or loose wires (FIG. 7-36). If the switch pops and cracks when turned on, replace it. Often a broken lever spring or defective switch has no leverage when turned off or on. A switch with high resistance across the terminals indicates worn or burned contacts. Replace with the original part number.

Check for worn brushes or open field coils by measuring motor continuity at the motor terminals. Remove brushes for inspection. The motor may be dismantled to check for an open winding or broken wires at the brush terminals. For larger motors, it might be best to return it to the nearest service center for repair. Make sure repairing the motor does not cost more than a new tool. (TABLE 7-1).

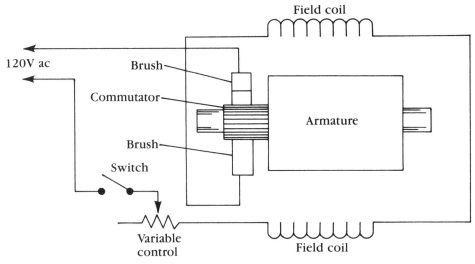

7-35 The wiring circuit of the bench sander.

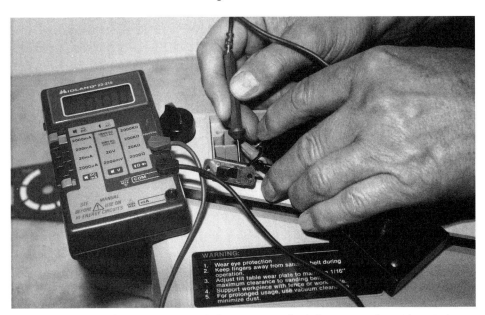

7-36 Connect ohmmeter across switch contacts to check for open or burned contacts.

POWER STAPLER

The electric stapling gun is a useful and versatile tool. Be careful when using it, however: These staples come out with great driving force and can accidentally injure you or others. Do not point the staple end towards anyone. Keep the on/off trigger locked when not in use (FIG. 7-37). Only remove the lock when stapling, then lock it again.

Inside the stapler

To take apart the electric power stapler for inspection or repair, first remove the body screws. Retrieve the nuts on the other side. Remove the washers so the two plastic pieces can come apart. Pull the long pins out with a pair of pliers. Carefully remove the top plastic lid. Be careful not to lose the two small steel slotted pieces (FIG. 7-38).

The staple is driven by a sheet of steel, the same size as the top of the stapler. The plunger hits the staple and drives it into the work, and the returning spring returns the metal plunger out of the solenoid winding.

Troubleshooting

If the staple gun will not fire, suspect a defective switch or fuse. A fuse is enclosed in the ac black tube shrinkage enclosure. The switch is a special type and must be replaced with the original part number (FIG. 7-39). Check the diodes on the pc board using the digital multimeter. Do not overlook the possibility of a broken cord where it enters the handle or at the three-prong plug.

Table 7-1. Troubleshooting Chart for Belt Sander

Problem	*Cause and Remedy*
Motor will not start	1. Check ac plug and cord 2. Check for open circuit fuse 3. Are other tools working on the same circuit? 4. Safety and off/on switch 5. Inspect brushes
Motor rotating with no belt rotation	1. Check belt tension lever 2. Broken belt
Excessive sawdust in housing	1. Clean out periodically—use shop vac 2. Clean up sawdust around the bench sander
Smoking motor	1. Sander has run too long—allow it to cool down and try again 2. If motor smokes immediately, check for worn brushes, shorted field winding, and grounded windings
Belt does not track	1. Check tension lever or rollers 2. If possible, set belt at slow speeds 3. Defective belt

7-37   Keep the on/off trigger of the staple gun locked at all times. Release it only when ready to staple.

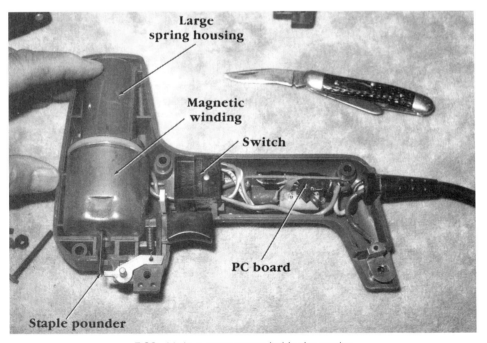

7-38   Various components inside the stapler.

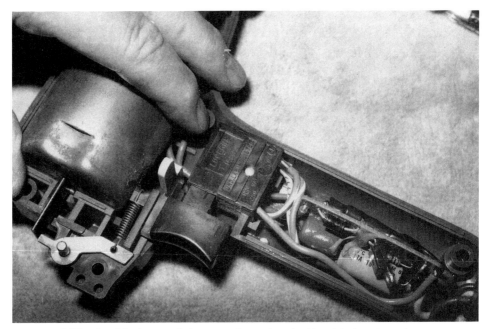

7-39 Special trigger switches must be replaced with original part numbers.

Make sure the switch, pc board, and cord are in the right grooves before replacement. The plastic cover must fit exactly over the metal plunger and down inside the plastic container. Slip the black staple holder in place and replace the top cover. The short screw fits in the top end of the plastic handle.

GLUE GUN

The electric glue gun allows 60-second bonding for repairing and constructing projects. With the trigger control, the exact amount of adhesive can be applied in the right spot. The gun uses glue sticks which melt into an adhesive that, when it dries again, forms a strong bond. The nozzle may be changed for various adhesives and job requirements.

For inspection or repair, remove the screws and take off the top cover (FIG. 7-40). The heating element in the glue gun is activated when the tool is plugged into an ac receptacle. The continuity resistance across the ac plug is around 85 to 90 ohms. A metallic thermostat located beside the metal heating body controls the temperature (FIG. 7-41). The pistol trigger only advances the glue; it does not shut the glue gun off or on.

Troubleshooting

Suspect a defective thermostat or open heater winding if there is no continuity measurement across the ac plug. Remove the screw type thermostat connector and check if either unit is open. Replace the thermostat unit if open. If a replacement cannot be found, eliminate it from the circuit, but then watch glue gun carefully for overheating. If you have problems with a glue gun that is used extensively, suspect a broken cord, either at the plug or where it is clamped together at the pistol end.

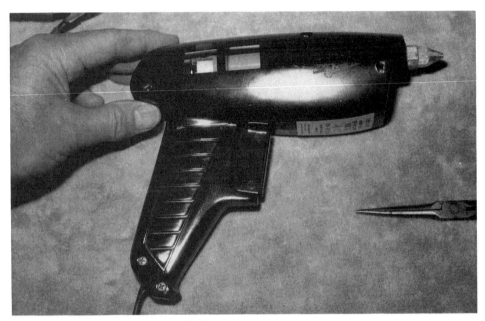

7-40   Electric glue gun.

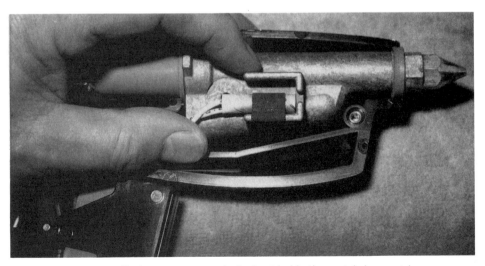

7-41   A metallic thermostat controls the heat inside the metal glue container.

The metal glue guide slides along a plastic track, which receives pressure from the trigger assembly. Clean out the glue slide when it will not move (FIG. 7-42). Pull up the trigger and clean out all dust and debris. Suspect a broken spring if the trigger assembly becomes stuck.

7-42 The metal glue guide assembly slides along a plastic track, which receives pressure from the trigger assembly.

The tool must be plugged in for 3 or 4 minutes before the adhesive is melted to change nozzles. If you want to change nozzles, use a wrench to remove the old one and simply screw in a new one. Do not touch hot nozzles. Allow the new nozzle to heat several minutes before using it.

PENCIL ENGRAVER

The pencil engraver is a handy tool you can use to mark all your tools with your name or identification number. This will be of help if they are ever stolen (FIG. 7-43). It will also help identify your tools when you are working with other people. You can permanently mark wood, plastic, glass, aluminum, copper, brass, lead, ceramics, stone, iron, and many other materials. These markings will not rub off or fade.

Troubleshooting

To take off the top cover for inspection and repair, first remove one screw and the front ring (FIG. 7-44). Be careful: The nozzle and washer might pop off because they are spring-loaded. Place a piece of tape over the end to hold them in place while checking out the coil and switch.

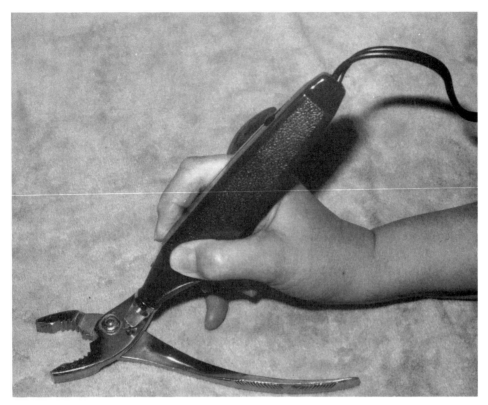

7-43 Identify your tools with this pencil engraver to prevent theft.

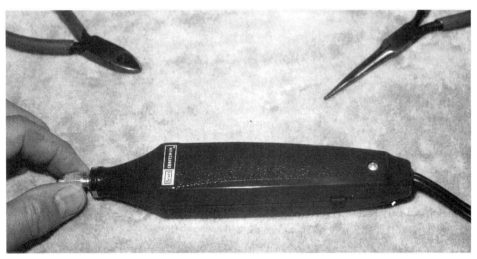

7-44 Remove one screw and metal ferrule band at the engraving end of tool to take off the top cover.

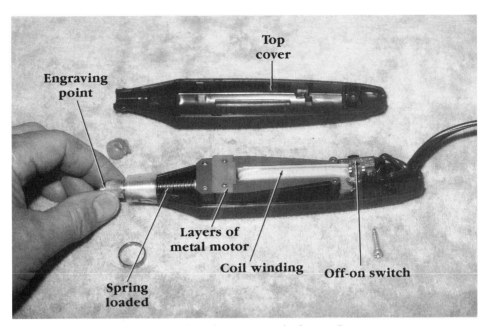

7-45 Internal view of components in the pencil engraver.

Although not much can go wrong with this tool because there are so few parts, if you do have a problem, first inspect the cord and plug for possible breaks in the wiring. Take a continuity test across the ac plug with the switch on. If the resistance is high or there is no reading, suspect a defective motor, switch, and cord.

Suspect a dirty switch or broken cord if the tool runs intermittently. Replace the defective switch. Measure the coil resistance at the end of the coil. This coil has a high resistance because it is wound with very fine wire. If the engraving point does not seem to vibrate as it should, suspect dirt accumulation between the vibrating piece and motor assembly. Simply brush out all dirt and filings (FIG. 7-45).

Chapter **8**

Medium power tools

Most of the medium power tools are portable units. The belt sander, router, sander/polisher, power circular saw, ½-inch speed drill, power plane, and the electric yard trimmer can be classified as portable power tools. The miter power saw, cutoff saw, and electric scroll saw are fastened to the workbench (FIG. 8-1).

These medium tools are serviced, like other power tools with universal motors. All of these tools have an armature with commutator and brushes. Portable power tools have trigger type switch handles for easy shut-off and operation. Often, two hands are required to operate each power tool.

See TABLE 8-1 for a troubleshooting guide.

PORTABLE BELT SANDER

This portable sander uses a 3-inch sanding belt (FIG. 8-2). Long bolts and nuts hold the body together. To gain access to the brushes for inspection, remove the plastic slotted circle and fiber spacers (FIG. 8-3). The brushes are found in each side of the motor. If excessive arcing is a problem, check the brushes for excess oil, broken ends and improper tension. Always remove the brushes before disassembling the sander.

Remove the body screws to take off the top cover of the sander (FIG. 8-4). Be careful not to lose the corresponding nuts. The belt may be loaded by pushing the front roller inward until it locks. If the motor operates but there is no belt action, remove three screws to get at the fiber tread belt. If the belt is broken, replace it (FIG. 8-5). Clean off the gear pulley and brush out excess dust before replacing the belt.

When the cover is removed, notice the fan blade and ball bearing at the motor end (FIG. 8-6). Pull out the armature and fan blade assembly from the field coil to inspect the armature and commutator. Replace the ac switch with the original because it is a specific type (FIG. 8-7). Brush out all dirt and dust from the roller assembly after repairing and lubricating the motor bearings.

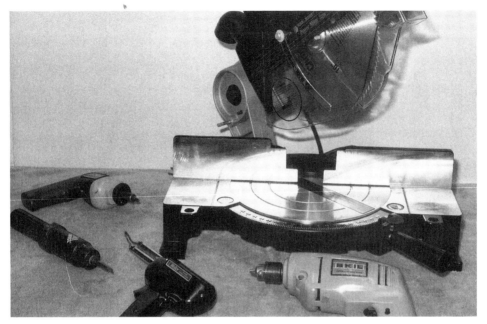

8-1 A medium size power tool: The electric miter saw.

Table 8-1. Troubleshooting Chart for Medium Power Tools

Problem	*Cause and Remedy*
Motor will not run	1. Check if ac plug and cord are open 2. Measure ac voltage at switch and white wire connection 3. Check continuity of motor winding with ohmmeter 4. Check electrolytic capacitor with tester or arcing test
Excessive vibration	1. Make sure saw is level and bolted to the bench 2. Improper mounting surface 3. Check for loose worktable—tighten table lock 4. Check for loose motor—tighten motor mounting bolts
Breaking blades	1. Poor tension—reajust table tension 2. Feeding material that is too large, too quickly 3. Use proper blades—narrow blades for thin wood and wide blades for thick wood
Blade not following pattern	1. Check for proper blade holder alignment 2. Loosen cap screws—realign blade holders and retighten
Intermittent operation	1. Check cord with ac meter at the motor terminals—flex ac cord 2. Check on/off switch 3. Check for grease in the switch or bad contacts 4. Motor has dirty starting contacts or connections

8-2   Side view of a portable belt sander with pistol grip operation and enclosed motor assembly.

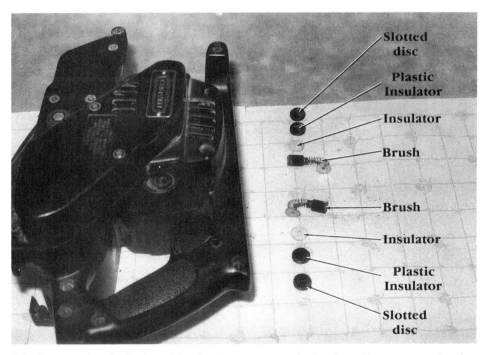

8-3   Remove the plastic slotted brush disc to remove the brushes. Always remove brushes before disassembling sander.

8-4 Remove external screws to take off the top cover.

8-5 Remove three small bolts to reach the tread belt, which rotates the belt at the bottom of sander.

8-6   The end ball bearing with cover removed. The armature assembly may be pulled from body assembly.

8-7   Replace ac switch with the original part number when the tool has a special type of trigger switch.

ROUTER

The router is a versatile power tool that can perform various functions: deep cutting, edge forming, groove cutting, and other specialized jobs (FIG. 8-8). The plunge routers are designed for speed, accuracy, and convenience in cabinet work, routing, fluting, dovetails, inlay work and decorative edges. Plunge routers allow interior cuts with ease, while the regular router must be tapped at an angle and sometimes chews up the material.

8-8 A bottom view of the router. Note the collet or chuck that holds the cutting tool. The diameter of bit shank must be the same size as the inside diameter of collet.

If the router is hard to control, heats up, runs very slowly, and leaves imperfect cuts, suspect improper direction feed. You can overload the motor if you feed material too quickly, use a dull bit, or make too large a cut at one pass. Alternatively, friction burns can result from feeding the router too slowly. Always feed smoothly and steadily without forcing. Feed the router so the blade turns into the work.

Remove the flat screws to reach the fan blade and armature assembly. Remove the flat screws and take off the end plate to reach the brushes and armature surface (FIG. 8-9). Check the cord, switch, and field coils with the digital multimeter.

Brush the dust out of the air vents and plunger springs. Keep tools clean by wiping with a soft cloth. Keep solvents such as gasoline and ammonia, as well as strong cleaning agents away from the plastic parts. Most routers have sealed ball bearings, so lubrication might not be required. Keep router bits clean by soaking in solvent, but remove ball bearing assembly beforehand.

8-9 Remove two flat screws to take off the end plate to inspect the motor brushes. Here they are housed inside the white plastic parts.

Take care of your router bits and keep them sharp. You might be able to sharpen them yourself, but it is best to take them to a professional. Router bits are not cheap.

SANDER/POLISHER

The sander/polisher is used for flat, large surfaces, such as cars or trucks (FIG. 8-10). Usually this tool is double-insulated, with two separate layers of material between the electrical system and operator, for added safety. The tool is grounded with a three-prong plug. Polish on low speed only, sand on high.

Clean off plastic parts with mild soap and a soft cloth. Do not lubricate the ball bearings. Inspect the bearings at least every 2 years under normal use.

Suspect a defective cord, switch, or brushes when the tool is dead. Take a quick ohmmeter continuity reading across the ac plug with switch at 3.7 ohms. Unplug the tool when taking continuity measurements.

Remove the body screws to gain access to the switch and brushes. Notice how the brushes are mounted for easy replacement (FIG. 8-11). This unit has a ball bearing on the front end and a sleeve bearing at the rear.

CIRCULAR SAW

The circular power saw operates at speeds up to 4600 RPM and pulls from 6.5 to 13 amps of current. It has changeable blades. The safety guard may be raised with a small side lever (FIG. 8-12).

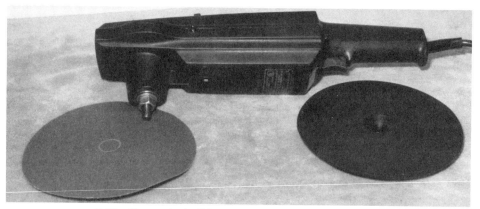

8-10   The sander/polisher may be used on any flat surface.

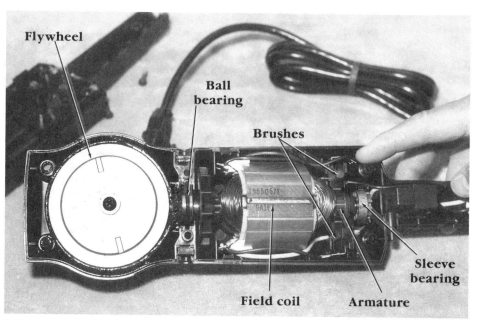

8-11   Inspect the bearings and gear assembly with the unit open. Notice how easily the brushes can be replaced.

   To repair or inspect the tool, remove the body screws to release the cover of the motor assembly and the handle. The saw blade may be exchanged or removed by unscrewing the arbor bolt with a socket wrench (FIG. 8-13). To remove the end piece, undo the screws and pull out the plastic piece with two round rubber stoppers. The brush holders fit in a slotted area and are held into position with these rubber stoppers. You can now pull the brush holders out for inspection and replacement (FIG. 8-14).

8-12 The circular saw.

8-13 Remove the arbor bolt to remove the blade.

8-14 To inspect brushes, remove two screws in plastic end piece. The brush holder can be pulled upward to remove brushes.

THE ¹/₂-INCH SPEED DRILL

The ½-inch speed drill will accept larger drill bits, operate for longer periods, and is designed for larger jobs than the smaller drills (FIG. 8-15). This drill has high-temperature magnet wire for the field coils, oil-impregnated ball thrust bearings, precision heavy-tooth gears, and a heavy wall housing. With the extended handle, more power can be exerted against the body of the drill. The tool has a reversing lever. The trigger switch serves as off/on switch and variable speed control. Drill speeds may vary from 0 to 500 RPM and a fixed 640 RPM. The ⅓ horsepower motor pulls from 6 to 8 amps with the variable speed.

Remove the slotted plastic at the rear of the motor to inspect or replace the motor brushes (FIG. 8-16). Remove the screws at the front of the drill to remove armature and gear assembly (FIG. 8-17). Make sure the brushes are removed before pulling the armature from the handle assembly (FIG. 8-18). Pull the armature out of the gear box and clean up if needed. The gear box should be lubricated with a light grease before replacement (FIG. 8-19). Remove the screws in the handle to check the switch assembly and power cord.

Safety

In addition to basic power tool safety, here are additional safety rules to follow when using a large heavy-duty drill.

- Always unplug the drill when attaching and changing accessories. Remove the key before starting up the drill.

- Use the correct drill bits. For wood, use twist drill, spade, or power auger bits. For metal, use high-speed twist drill bits. For masonry, use carbide tipped bits.
- Center punch the point to be drilled before drilling to prevent slippage. This is not needed with low-speed variable drills.
- Make sure the material to be drilled is well anchored or clamped. Use wood blocks between the clamp and the piece you are working on to prevent damage to the material.
- Do not put excessive pressure on the drill to stop it; you can overheat the motor or burn the tip of the drill bit. Use medium pressure and drill straight in. When drilling large holes, first drill a smaller pilot hole.
- Keep drill bits sharp to prevent wood damage or burning of drill tips. Sharpen the bit or use a new one when it begins to smoke and burn the material.
- If the drill stalls, shut it off at once. Do not click the trigger switch off and on to release the bit; you could damage or overheat the drill.
- To prevent stalling or damage to the material, reduce pressure on the body of the drill.
- To prevent jamming, keep the motor running when pulling the bit out of a long drilled hole. Pull the bit out frequently to clean off material when drilling long or deep holes.
- Use a cutting lubricant such as cutting oil or lard when drilling metal. Some manufacturers recommend using kerosene as a lubricant when drilling aluminum: Be careful if you plan to use kerosene, because it is flammable. Do not use any liquid when drilling cast iron or brass.
- Use a metal handle to steady and aim the drill, to keep it straight while drilling difficult holes.
- Release the lock switch before pulling the plug on the drill; damage or injury could result when plugging in the drill the next time.

MITER SAW

The miter saw can cut wood, composition board, aluminum, and plastics with the proper saw blade. It can be used for straight cuts or miters, and works especially well for cutting molding and trim (FIG. 8-20). As with all saws, keep hands and fingers from the kerf plate. Practically any type of angle can be cut on the miter saw. Keep the blade parallel and at a right angle with the fence and table.

Most miter saws have self-lubricating bearings. Check the bearings every 2 years under normal usage. Clean off the plastic case with mild soap and a soft cloth. Apply paste or spray wax to the base and rotary table.

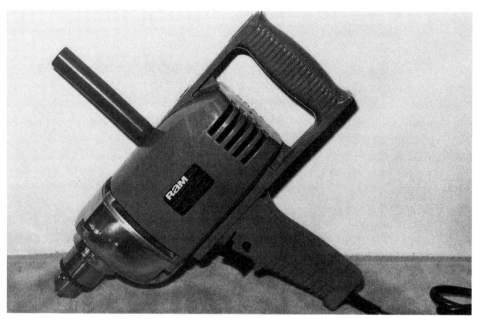

8-15 The ¹/₂-inch speed drill can accept larger bits, and more power can be exerted against the body of the drill with the extended handle.

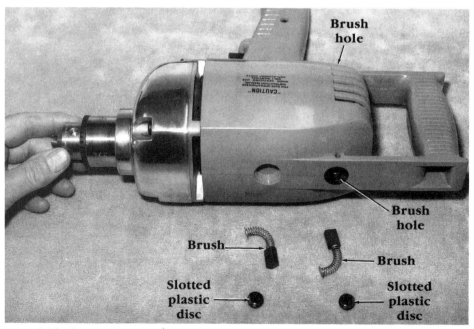

8-16 Remove the slotted discs at the end of the drill to reach the motor brushes.

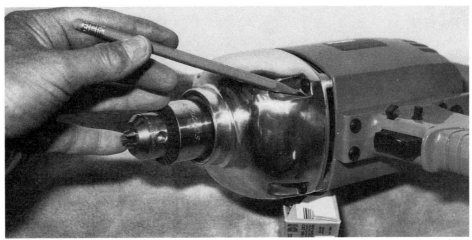

8-17 Remove the screws at the front of the drill to take off the armature and gear assembly.

8-18 Pull out the armature and gear assembly after brushes are removed.

If the unit will not operate, use the ohmmeter to take a continuity reading at 12.6 ohms. Make sure switch is turned on and not plugged into the outlet. Remove the body screws and take off the motor housing assembly. Inspect the brushes and bearings while the motor is open (FIG. 8-21). Remove arbor nut and collar to pull off drill saw blade (FIG. 8-22). The arbor nut turns counterclockwise when mounting new saw blade. Remove the guard before installing a new saw blade.

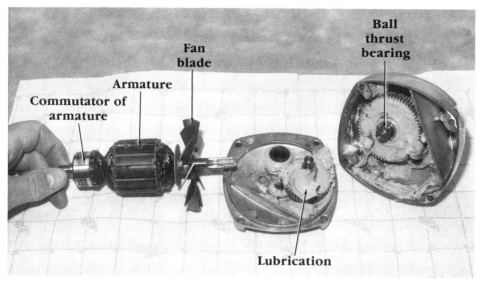

8-19 Remove front gear box. Lubricate with a light grease.

8-20 The miter power saw can accurately cut molding, trim work, picture frame material, and aluminum or plastic tubing at practically any angle.

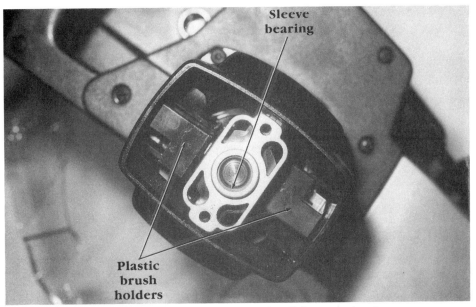

8-21 Remove the body screws to take off the motor housing.

8-22 Before attempting to replace saw blade, remove the blade guard, arbor nut, and collar.

POWER PLANE

The electric plane should be operated on a flat surface. Move the tool slowly into the work and maintain downward pressure to keep the plane flat at the beginning and end of the work surface (FIG. 8-23). Make sure the motor is at full speed before beginning to plane.

8-23   Keep equal pressure on the plane, beginning to end of the work surface.

Clean up the tool with mild soap and a soft cloth. Be careful not to get liquid down inside the motor or belt openings. Do not immerse tool in liquid. Brush out dirt and sawdust from the vents.

Remove the body screws and take off the side piece to gain access to the belt assembly (FIG. 8-24). The motor pulley rotates the drive belt and cutting blades. Remove screws on the other side of the tool to inspect the armature (FIG. 8-25). Remove the body screws that will allow you to open up the whole plane assembly. Inspect the brushes, cord, plug, and field coils. If there is no motor rotation, use the digital multimeter to take a continuity measurement and locate possible open circuits (FIG. 8-26). The reading should be around 3.1 ohms.

WEED TRIMMER

The electric weed trimmer may come in small (8-inch), medium (10-inch) and large (12-inch) sizes. This tool uses rapidly rotating nylon cutting line to trim weeds and grass (FIG. 8-27). With earlier models of weed trimmers, there was often a problem releasing the nylon line. With modern models, you usually simply need to tap the cap underneath the tool, which releases from 1 to 2½ inches of cord (FIG. 8-28). When making inspections or repairs, first remove the screws that hold the bottom plastic guard plate. Then remove the screws of the motor body and plastic handle to check the brushes and motor (FIG. 8-29). The brushes are held in plastic holders with a tension spring.

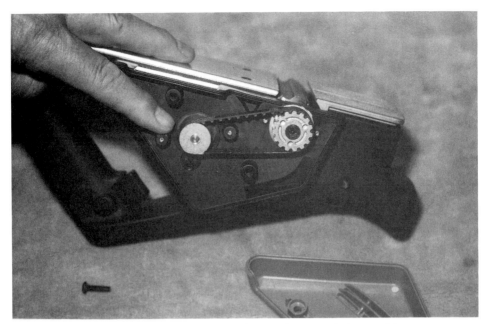

8-24 Remove two screws to inspect the motor belt assembly.

8-25 Remove two screws to inspect armature and brushes.

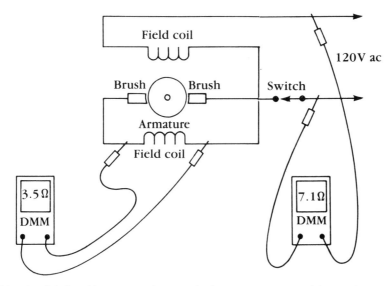

8-26   Use the digital multimeter to take a continuity measurement and locate the open circuit.

8-27   Electric weed trimmer. A nylon cutting line rotates rapidly to trim weeds and grass.

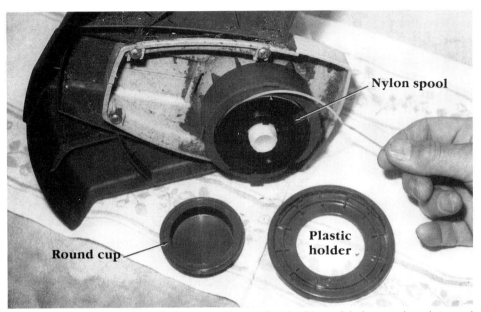

8-28 The nylon line can be pulled out to add more line. In this model, the round cup is tapped to release 1 to 2 1/2 inches of line.

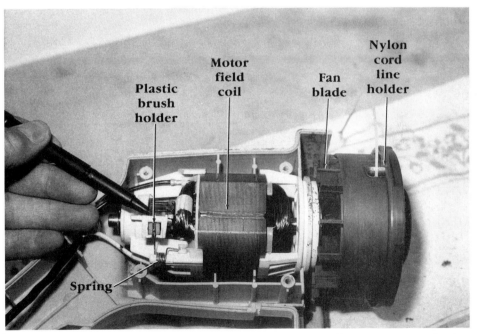

8-29 Remove screws in motor body and plastic handle assembly to reach the motor. Brushes are held in the plastic holders with a tension spring.

Safety

In addition to basic power tool safety, follow these steps for safe use of the weed trimmer:

- Always wear a pair of goggles or face shield while operating the weed trimmer; the fast-rotating line might throw objects outward.

- Keep bystanders at least 25 feet away from the weed cutting operation. Shut off the tool if someone approaches.

- Inspect the entire tool, especially the bottom area, for broken or cracked parts. Replace with exact part numbers.

- Keep your feet and body away from the trimmer head. Remove ac plug before working on or adjusting weed trimmer.

- Keep cutting head and shield clean. Wipe off after using with damp cloth or sponge. Do not set the tool in water.

- Use Number 18 AWG wire extension cord (up to 50 feet) or Number 16 AWG (up to 100 feet) to operate the weed trimmer.

GRASS EDGER

This electric edger may be used as a trimmer, trencher, bevel cutter, or edger around sidewalks or buildings (FIG. 8-30). To rotate the edger downward for trenching and sidewalk edging, simply pull out on the black knob and turn the body with trimming blade down (FIG. 8-31).

Most service problems with the electric edger involve a bad ac plug connection, broken off/on switch, and motor brushes. This tool uses a universal motor that rotates the trim blade with a direct shaft. To reach the brushes and fan assembly, remove the screws at the top of the motor assembly (FIG. 8-32). Remove the screws to take off the end bell of the motor. Pull out the armature and end bearings for lubrication.

8-30 This electric edger may be used as a trimmer, trencher, bevel cutter, or edger.

8-31   Pull out on black knob to rotate the edger downward.

8-32   Remove the screws and pull off plastic top cover to reach the brushes.

SCROLL SAW

The scroll saw is ideal for a wide range of projects. It may be mounted on the workbench or a metal table (FIG. 8-33). The scroll saw blade can be moved into right, C-arm, or parallel positions. The average maximum depth cut is from 2 to 2 1/2 inches. Some scroll saws have variable electronic speed controls. This table may be tilted to one side for 45-degree cuts (FIG. 8-34). After tilting to the desired position, check the angle gauge and lock the table in place with the large knob.

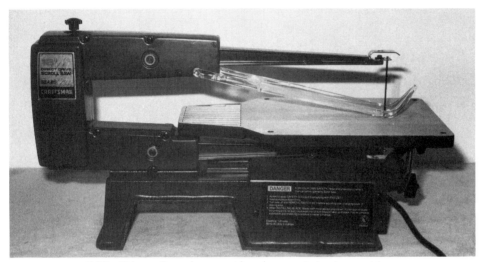

8-33 This scroll saw has a cast-iron base and aluminum table.

Lubricate the arm bearings after 10 hours of use when the saw is new. Then re-oil every 50 hours, or whenever a squeaky noise is heard from the bearings. Plastic cups are provided to place oil into the bearings. Snap oil-filled cups over the end bearings. The saw may be turned on its side to oil the bearings if cups are not provided. Use SAE 20 motor oil (FIG. 8-35).

Remove the screws to gain access to the switch and cord assembly, then remove the screws to take off the motor end cover as shown in FIG. 8-36. Mark the end belt of the motor before removing the screws to pull out the armature for inspection. Notice that the motor starting capacitor is located inside the switch assembly. A yellow start button is inserted into the switch assembly so the scroll arm can be operated (FIG. 8-37). Remove the yellow plastic piece for safety and to lock off the switch.

When removing or installing blades on the scroll saw, always make sure the switch is off or the power plug pulled. Loosen tension on the blade by rotating the tension knob—usually counterclockwise—at least 2 full turns. Pull the blade forward and lift it through the hole in the table. Sometimes pushing down on the upper arm of the scroll saw will help. The teeth of the saw blade should be pointed downward. Install the blade through the hole. Hook the blade pin in the pin recess of the bottom and top blade holder. Carefully tighten the blade tension by turning the knob in the reverse direction. Rotate the tool by hand to check that the blade is installed correctly.

HEDGE TRIMMER

The hedge trimmer is a handy tool, but can also be a dangerous one if not operated correctly. Keep hands away from the blades. Do not overreach when trimming; keep hands on the handles. Do not use the tool in wet conditions. Make sure the tool is off before setting it down (FIG. 8-38).

Self-lubricating bearings are used in most hedge trimmers. Lubricate the sleeve bearings with light oil after 2 or 3 years of operation. File out any knicks in the blade if they prevent normal operation. Clean off the plastic case and motor assembly with mild soap and a cloth.

Remove the body screws, as shown in FIG. 8-39, to check the brushes. Remove the side screws to inspect the switch and blade assembly. Check the continuity of cord, switch, armature, and field coils with the digital multimeter (FIG. 8-40). It should measure a total of 20 to 25 ohms across the plug.

8-34 The working table may be tilted to one side, up to a 45-degree angle. Check the angle gauge and lock the table in place with the large black knob.

8-35 Lubricate the arm bearings approximately every 50 hours. Plastic cups are provided to place SAE 20 motor oil into the bearings. The saw may be turned on its side to oil these bearings if cups are lost or not used.

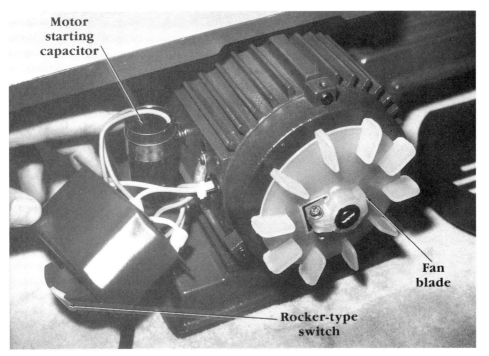

8-36 Remove these screws to reach the switch and cord assembly. The motor starting capacitor is located under this cover.

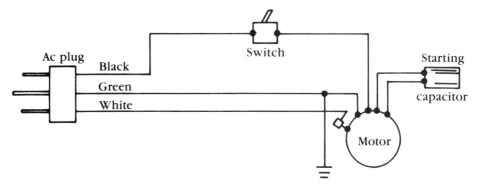

8-37 The motor wiring connections located under the switch container.

8-38 Turn off the hedge trimmer before setting it down.

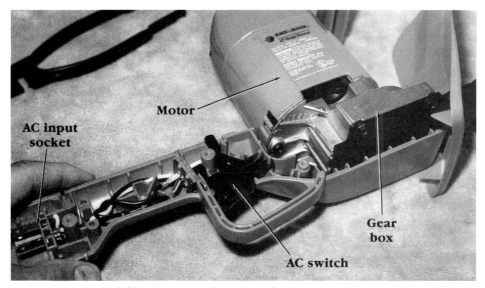

8-39 Remove these screws to inspect the brushes.

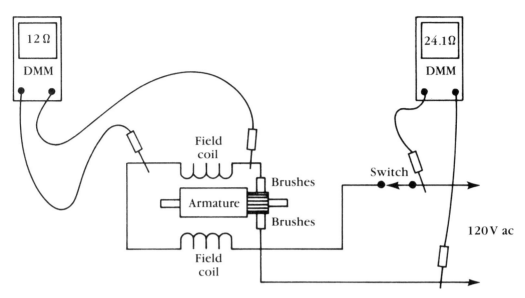

8-40 Use the digital multimeter to check the continuity of cord, switch, armature, and field coils.

Chapter **9**

Large power tools

Large power tools can either mount onto a bench or be freestanding (FIG. 9-1). These tools include the miter, radial or table saw, drill press, sander, and molder/planer.

Large power tools can be operated from an internal or external motor. Many of the tools are fused with 15- or 20-amp fuses, although they can pull more current from the power line. Each tool on the bench should be grounded with a three-prong plug.

SAFETY

- Read the instruction manual before operating power tool. Learn the specific hazards of the tool.
- Keep guards in place and in working order.
- Ground all tools. Use a three-prong plug or wire directly to fuse box ground.
- Remove all adjusting keys and wrenches. Make it a habit to double check where keys and wrenches are before starting up the power tool.
- Keep work area clean. Cluttered benches and areas invite accidents.
- Don't use power tools in damp or wet areas. Keep them out of the rain.
- Keep work area well lighted.
- Keep children and visitors away while working with power tools.
- Padlock tools or master switches, or remove starter keys.
- Don't force the tool. It will operate safer and do a better job, if used as designed.
- Do not wear loose clothing, gloves, rings, bracelets, or neckties that could be caught in moving parts.

- Always wear eye protection. Also wear a dust mask, if work causes a lot of dust.
- Secure work with clamps or a vise when possible.
- Don't overreach. Keep proper footing and balance.
- Keep tools in top shape.
- Disconnect tools before servicing or changing blades and bits.
- Make sure switch is off before plugging in the tool.
- Check for damaged parts. If the tool is not operating properly, check for damaged moving part.
- Feed work into a blade or cutter, against the direction of rotation.
- Never leave the tool running unattended. Turn off the power, and do not leave the power tool until it comes to a complete stop.

Delta Corp.

9-1 Large power tools: miter saw, radial arm saw, drill press, sander, and molder/planer.

UPRIGHT BAND SAW

The band saw can be attached to a bench, or be freestanding (FIG. 9-2). The saw can be powered with a universal or induction motor. Most large stationary saws have induction motors—¼ to ½ horsepower.

9-2 The band saw can set upon the bench or be freestanding. These band saws may be powered with universal or induction motors.

Many band saw problems are related to a defective cord and plug, ac switch, or motor.

To open the band saw, remove the four round nuts, as shown in FIG. 9-3. Check the large rotating wheels. Often wheel tension control is at the top of the band saw, with a tracking adjustment to the side (FIG. 9-4). Use the ohmmeter to test the ac cord, switch, and motor terminals. Check the lubricating wells and cups for adequate lubrication of ball and sleeve bearings (FIG. 9-5).

Always operate the band saw with the throat plate in place (FIG. 9-6). Otherwise, small pieces of wood can lodge between table and saw blade and snap the blade.

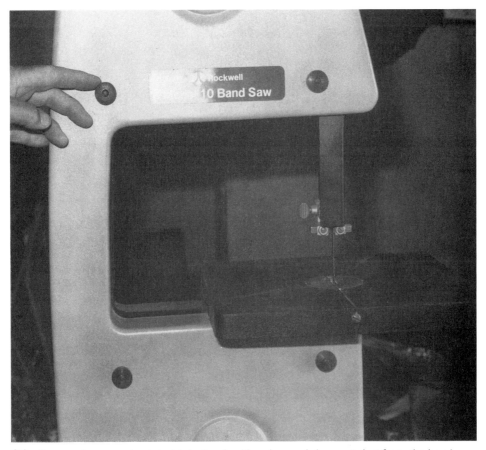

9-3   Remove four round nuts to lubricate wheel bearings and clean out dust from the band saw.

TABLE SAW

The table saw consists of a motor and belt, tilting arbor, circular blade, and table (FIG. 9-7). The motor rotates the arbor by belt or may be directly driven. Most of the motor and arbor bearings are ball bearings, with a few sleeve bearings. Lubricate bearings with Number 20 SAE oil. Place the oil in caps or wells beside motor bearings (FIG. 9-8).

To remove and replace the saw blade, remove the two screws holding the arbor plate down. Remove the plate. Unloosen the large arbor nut. Rotate the end wrench towards the cutting rotation of saw blade. Prevent the saw blade from turning with a piece of scrap wood. Now remove the nut, washer, and saw blade. Replace the saw blade with cutting edge downward. Tighten the arbor nut. Brush out any dust before replacing the aluminum plate. Readjust height and angle of cutting, if needed. Always keep the safety guard in place while operating the bench saw.

Blade tracking

Tension adjuster

9-4 Adjust the large wing nut at the top of the saw for correct tension. Adjust the side wing nut for proper tracking of the saw blade.

If there is a problem with the motor, use the ohmmeter to check the ac switch, cord, and overload protectors. Besides electrical malfunctions, mechanical problems can occur with the mechanical blade height and tilt adjustments (FIG. 9-9). Sometimes sawdust will fall into the screw mechanism, causing binding and difficult operation. Prevent problems by lubricating these mechanical mechanisms with light oil.

Improper belt alignment can cause the motor to slow down and can also cause excessive belt wear. A coat of beeswax prevents the belt from slipping when sawing hard or thick wood pieces. Besides cleaning the tabletop, clean the motor and undercarriage of excessive sawdust. Wipe off metal parts with oily rag. Spray or paste wax on the cast iron table helps prevent rust (FIG. 9-10).

BENCH GRINDER

Bench grinders come in different sizes. The large bench grinder with 6-inch wheels and speeds up to 3600 RPM can do heavy grinding jobs. Large grinders are powered by ¼ to ⅓ horsepower induction motors (FIG. 9-11). Most of the new grinders have eyeshields, but always wear goggles to protect your eyes when using any type of grinder. Replace grinding wheels when they become cracked, irregular, or worn down. Sometimes the irregular wheels can be cleaned up with a grinding wheel dresser (FIG. 9-12).

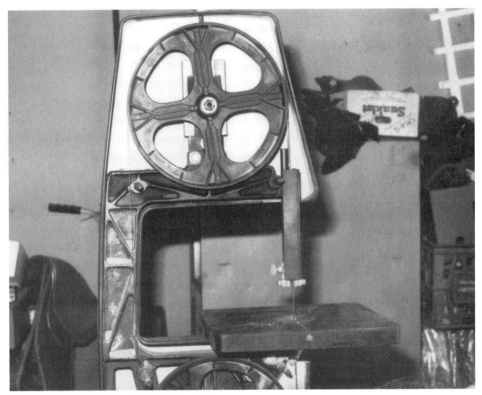

9-5 Lubricate the wells and cups of the sleeve bearings on the rotating blade wheels.

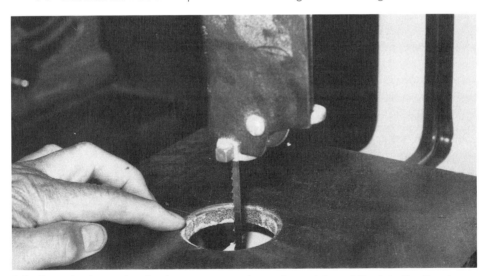

9-6 Keep the throat plate in place to prevent pieces of wood from falling into the throat area and snapping the blade.

9-7 The table saw consists of a tilting arbor, motor and belt, circular blade, and table.

9-8 Lubricate the motor sleeve bearings with Number 20 SAE oil. Place oil in cap or wells beside motor bearings.

9-9   Brush off sawdust along blade and tilting screws. Then apply a light coat of oil to keep long screws from rusting.

9-10   The original updated table saw with painted body and clean table.

9-11 This larger bench grinder with a 6-inch grinding wheel powered by a $^1/_3$ horsepower induction motor.

9-12 Use a wheel dresser if the grinding wheel becomes worn in places. Do not grind on the side of the wheels.

If the wheel begins to wobble, unloosen the nut holding the flange washer and rotate the wheel 90 degrees. Now retighten the nut and recheck the wheel. Rotate and readjust the wheel until most of the wobble disappears. Some wheels might have a little irregular movement, which is normal. Do not tighten the nut too much; excessive pressure can damage the wheel (FIG. 9-13). Most problems with the grinder are related to the switch, grinding wheels, and bearings. Grinders with roller ball bearings and induction motors cause very few problems.

9-13 Excessive pressure on the wheel nut can damage the wheel.

Safety

In addition to basic power tool safety rules, follow these specifically for the bench grinder:

- Always use guards and eyeshields, and wear a pair of safety goggles.
- Examine grinding wheels. If there are cracks or breaks, replace the wheel immediately.
- Do not overtighten wheel nuts; this could cause damage to the grinding wheel.
- Mount the grinder securely and bolt it to the workbench.
- Make sure grinder wheel is shut off and has stopped before making any kind of adjustments.

- To avoid personal injury, do not force the work against the grinder wheel.
- When replacing the grinding wheel, select the correct wheel for the speed of the grinder.

BENCH PLANER

The bench planer molds, saws, sands, and planes wood. Some units have an automatic feed while smaller units have a manual feed. The portable or bench planer may be operated with a self-contained motor or with a belt-driven motor that is mounted separately upon the bench (FIG. 9-14).

9-14　Bench wood planer with 1½ horsepower capacitor start motor. The motor is mounted separately.

In the molder/planer shown here, the heavy cast-iron lid is removed to get at the cutting blades (FIG. 9-15). The depth of the cut is controlled by a knob at the top that turns a large screw shaft. The planer is powered by a 1½ horsepower capacitor start motor. The electrolytic capacitor and cutout is located on top of the motor (FIG. 9-16).

Most problems occurring with any planer or molder are related to power switches, dull blades, and belt and motor problems. Keep the sliding bars and table free of rust with a coat of light oil.

9-15   Remove the heavy cast-iron lid to remove or change cutting blades in this bench molder.

9-16   The capacitor start motor has a thermal cutout, which protects the motor and can be reset if motor kicks out.

DRILL PRESS

The drill press comes in many different sizes: hand-held, bench, and floor models. Most drill presses have a ¼ to ¾ horsepower split-phase induction motor that is fastened to the rear head of the machine (FIG. 9-17).

9-17 This bench drill press has a rear-mounted ¼ horsepower motor with belt drive.

Wipe the table and all metal areas with oil or paste wax to prevent rusting. Apply paste wax upon surfaces that are stationary. Check the front bearings once a month if used constantly. Drop Number 20 SAE oil into the bearing slots. Check the motor oil cups twice per year. Make sure the belt is in line and that it does not slip (FIG. 9-18). Inspect the motor for worn or dry bearings if you hear a screeching, dry noise (FIG. 9-19).

9-18 The speed may be changed by placing the motor belt on another pulley. Keep belt in line for normal wear.

Motor shaft

End bell

Armature

Actuator

Metal end

Sleeve bearing

9-19 Inspect the motor bearings. Place oil in wells of sleeve bearings twice a year.

RADIAL ARM SAW

The radial arm saw operates somewhat like the miter and chop saws, except the whole saw assembly moves outward on a large arm. The radial arm saw is the shop workhorse and is used to cut large pieces of lumber. The saw can be mounted on a bench or be freestanding.

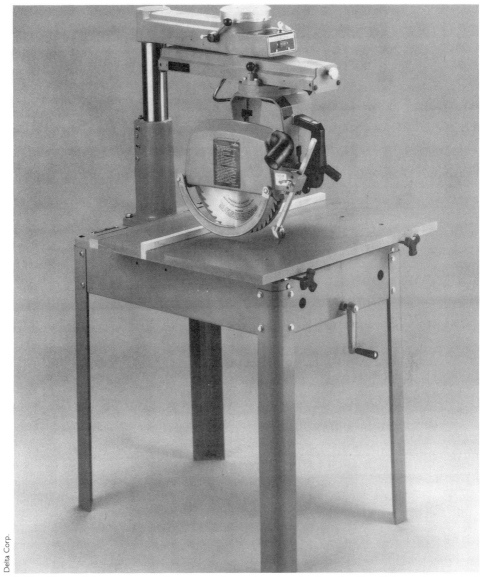

Delta Corp.

9-20   The radial arm saw may be mounted on a bench or be freestanding. This saw is mounted on its own stand.

Table 9-1. Single- and Three-Phase Motor Wires and Fuses

HP	SINGLE PHASE				THREE PHASE			
	115 VOLTS		230 VOLTS		200 - 230 VOLTS		460 VOLTS	
	WIRE SIZE	TIME LAG FUSE*	WIRE SIZE	TIME LAG FUSE*	WIRE SIZE	TIME LAG FUSE*	WIRE SIZE	TIME LAG FUSE*
1½	12	20	14	15	–	–	–	–
2	–	–	–	–	14	15	14	15

*Size fuse selected for branch circuit protection.
*Time lag fuse is not applicable in Canada.

Single-phase machines

The single-phase motor may be operated from 115 or 230 ac volts. A 1½- or 2-horsepower motor is connected with Number 12 wire and protected with a 20-amp fuse. The single-phase 230-volt motor may be connected with Number 14 wire and a 15-amp time lag fuse (TABLE 9-1). Make sure the green wire of the three-prong plug is grounded.

Three-phase machines

The three-phase radial saw motor may be wired for either 200, 230, or 460 volts. Have an electrician wire up these heavy, high-voltage motors. A magnetic motor starting box is located in these three-phase circuits. Three-phase motors may also be wired with Number 14 wire and fuse protected with a 15-amp time lag fuse.

Motor hookup

The motor hookup connections must be changed at the motor of either 115- or 230-volt single-phase machines (FIG. 9-21). The 115-volt manual single-phase motor circuit is shown in FIG. 9-22, and the 230-volt manual single-phase motor connections in FIG. 9-23.

Single-phase motor starter

The single-phase magnetic motor starter is comprised of an overload block, magnetic contactor, transformer, and start/stop station. The single-phase starter is comprised of a power circuit and a central circuit (FIG. 9-24). The heavy lines indicate the power lines that have larger gauge wire running to the motor. The main function of the control circuit is to start and stop the electric motor.

MOTOR CONNECTIONS FOR SINGLE PHASE RADIAL SAWS

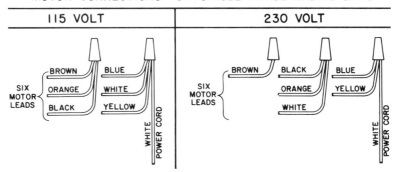

9-21 Single-phase 115- and 230-volt motor connections on the radial saw.

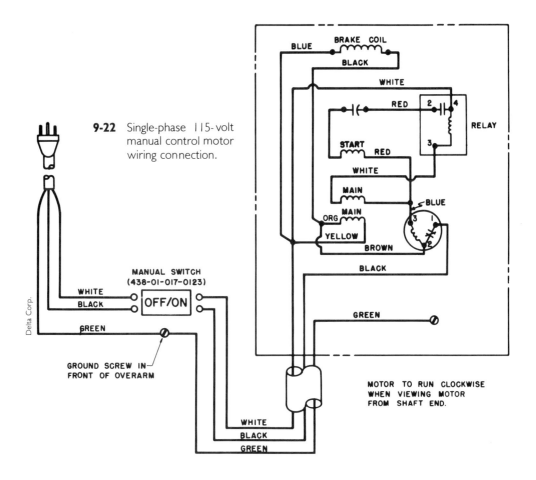

9-22 Single-phase 115-volt manual control motor wiring connection.

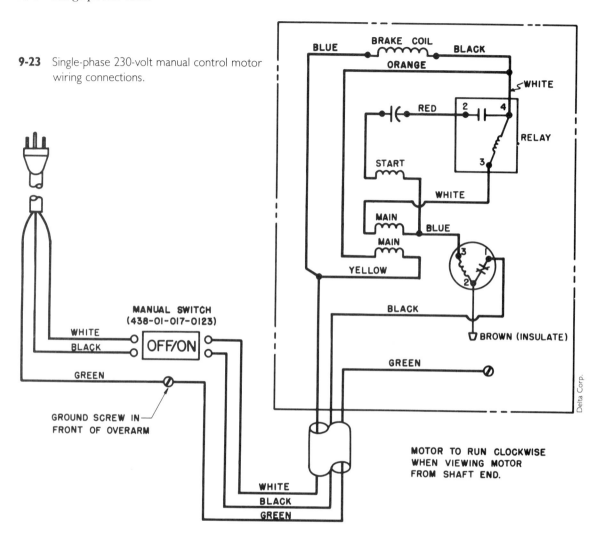

9-23 Single-phase 230-volt manual control motor wiring connections.

Three-phase motor starter

The three-phase motor starting circuit is somewhat like the single-phase starter, except three power lines operate the motor. The three-phase motor starter is comprised of the power circuit and control circuits (FIG. 9-25).

BENCH WOOD LATHE

The lathe is a tool used for wood turning. The material to be turned is rotated by a headstock spindle, which is driven by a motor on the lathe bed. The cutting tool lays on the tool rest and bites into the spinning wood (FIG. 9-26). The motor may be built in, mounted directly behind headstock, or mounted directly below the lathe. The motor may be ½, ¾, 1, or 1½ horsepower, depending upon the size of the lathe. The speed is usually controlled by a 3- to 5-step pulley. Figure 9-27 illustrates the parts of the lathe.

Check the direction of rotation of the wood lathe when installing the motor. The spur center must be turned counterclockwise when viewed from the tailstock end. Most wood lathes are operated with a 1725 RPM motor. Never use a motor with automatic thermal overload.

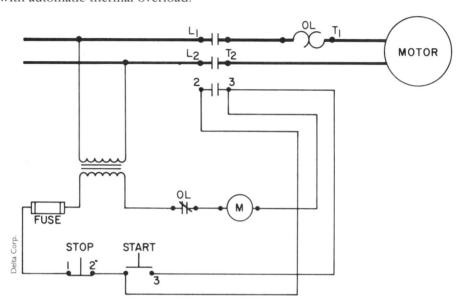

9-24   Schematic diagram of a single-phase magnetic motor starter.

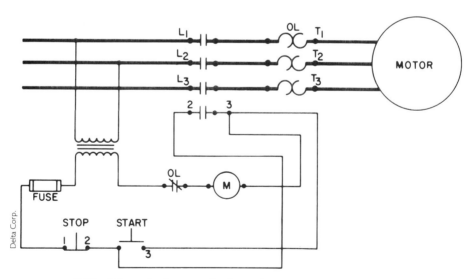

9-25   Schematic diagram of a three-phase magnetic motor starter.

9-26 The wood or material to be turned is rotated with a headstock spindle driven by a ¹/2 to I ¹/2 horsepower motor.

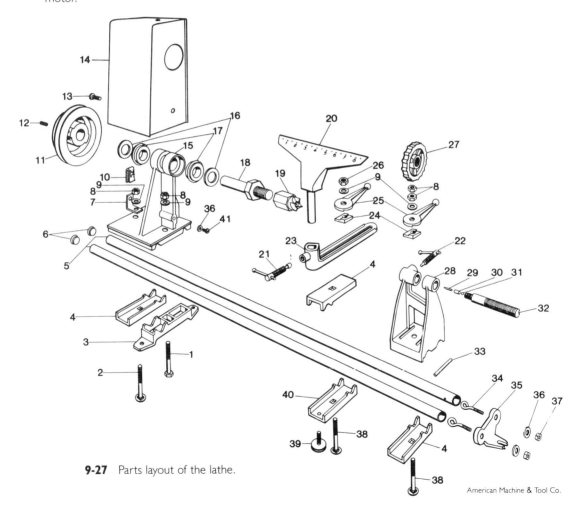

9-27 Parts layout of the lathe.

PARTS LIST

WHEN ORDERING REPAIR PARTS, ALWAYS GIVE THE FOLLOWING INFORMATION:

1. The PART NUMBER
2. The PART NAME

3. The MODEL NUMBER 2731 OR 2731B
4. The NAME of ITEM — LATHE

KEY NO.	PART NO.	DESCRIPTION	KEY NO.	PART NO.	DESCRIPTION
1	1763.00	3/8-16 x 2-1/2 Hex Head Cap Screw	21	E1278.00	Tee Rest Lock Assembly
2	1765.00	3/8-16 x 3 Carriage Bolt	22	E1278.10	Tail Spindle Lock Assembly
3	1228.00	Headstock Foot	23	1235.10	Tee Rest Holder
4	1231.00	Clamp (3 Req.)	24	1244.01	Cam Lock Arm Wedge (2 Req.)
5	1242.00	Bed Tube (2 Req.)	25	1245.01	Cam Lock Arm (2 Req.)
6	1253.00	Bed Tube Plug (2)	26	1781.20	3/8-16 MF 2-Way Lock Nut
7	1230.00	Hood Clip	27	1234.00	Tail Handwheel
8	1781.00	3/8-16 Hex Fin Jam Nut (4)	28	1225.00	Tailstock
9	1793.00	3/8 SAE Washer (4)	29	1248.00	Cup Center Point
10	1240.00	Headstock Hood Nut (Special)	30	1246.00	Cup Center
11	1355.00	Pulley 3/4 Bore, 3 Step	31	1247.00	Cup Center Ball
12	1738.01	5/16-18 x 1/2 Socket Set Screw	32	1233.00	Tail Spindle
13	1699.00	8-32 x 3/8 Round Head Machine Screw	33	1249.00	Tail End Cross Bar
14	1239.00	Headstock Hood	34	1250.00	Tail End Foot Eyebolt (2 Req.)
15	1227.0001	Headstock (Bronze Bearing)	35	1229.00	Tail End Foot
15	1227.0002	Headstock (Ball Bearing)	36	1789.00	1/4 SAE Washer (3 Req.)
16	1237.00	Thrust Washer (3/4 x 1-3/16 x 1/16) (2 Req.)	37	1773.00	1/4-20 Hex Nut (2 Req.)
17	1252.10	Bronze Bearing (2 Req.)	38	1766.00	3/8-16 x 3-3/4 Carriage Bolt (2 Req.)
17	1251.00	Ball Bearing (2 Req.)	39	1241.00	Tee Rest Support Foot
18	1232.00	Headstock Spindle	40	1231.0001	Tee Rest Clamp
19	1238.00	Spur Center	41	1715.00	1/4-20 x 1/2 Hex Head Cap Screw
20	1236.00	Tee Rest			

°Standard Hardware Items — May Be Purchased Locally.

This sheet is intended for instruction and repair parts only and is not a packing slip.
The parts shown and listed may include accessories not necessarily part of this tool.

9-27 Continued.

Lubricate the sleeve bearings with SAE 20 motor oil, the ball bearings with light motor grease. Check the oil well end bearings on larger horsepower motors at least once a year. The continuity of the motor, switch, and cord may be checked with the digital multimeter.

UPRIGHT BELT SANDER

The narrow upright belt sander mounts directly on the bench (FIG. 9-28). The small motor may be ⅕ to ⅓ horsepower, mounted right in the base unit. The metal table can tilt to 45°. The belt rotates directly from the motor pulley (FIG. 9-29).

Keep table and motor assembly clean at all times. Brush off fine sawdust with a large paintbrush. Check the belt bearings at least once a year. Wipe off table and metal parts with an oil and a soft cloth.

If the motor does not rotate, check the bench sander continuity. It should measure 2.6 ohms. If the tool runs intermittently, check the on/off switch and plug. Clean the switch contacts. If the switch is broken, replace it with the exact part number (FIG. 9-30).

AIR COMPRESSOR

Air compressors used in the shop or garage can either be portable or consist of a large tank mounted on wheels. The small compressor is ideal for spray painting and air tools (FIG. 9-31).

9-28 The upright belt sander may be mounted directly upon the bench.

When using the compressor follow the manufacturer's safety procedures as listed in the owner's manual. Be sure and drain the compressor tank after each use to prevent rust formation.

Compressor pump

The electric motor in the compressor pump provides power to keep the pistons moving. A piston inside the pump compresses air by moving left to right in the cylinder head of the air compressor. As the piston moves to the left, air enters the chamber through the intake valve. As the piston moves to the right, the intake valve closes and the piston compresses the air. The compressed air is sent through the outlet valve to the tank. Figure 9-32 illustrates the components of the air compressor.

9-29 The motor may be a ¹/5 to ¹/3 horsepower self-contained motor driving a motor pulley or gear assembly.

9-30 Replace the on/off switch with the original part number.

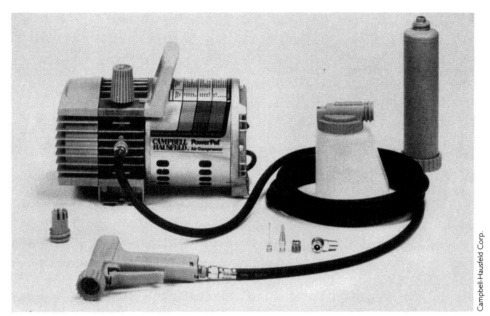

Campbell-Hausfeld Corp.

9-31   The air compressor may be portable or consist of a large tank mounted on wheels.

Regulator

The regulator allows control of the air pressure released at the base outlet. Turn the regulator knob clockwise to increase pressure and counterclockwise to decrease pressure. A full counterclockwise turn will shut off the flow of air completely.

ASME safety valve

This valve automatically releases air if the tank pressure exceeds the preset maximum. The valve is found on compressors with separate air tanks. Replace the valve if air leaks after the ring has been pulled, or if valve is stuck.

Maintenance

Check and clean filters after each use. If unit is used under dusty conditions or when spraying paint, keep it as far away from the work area as the air hose will allow, to avoid overspray and to keep dust from accumulating in the compressor unit. See TABLE 9-2 for a troubleshooting guide.

BENCH OR TABLE JOINTER

The bench or table jointer has a number of useful features. It can be used to bevel, taper, and joint pieces of wood (FIG. 9-33). However, the jointer may be a dangerous machine if not used properly.

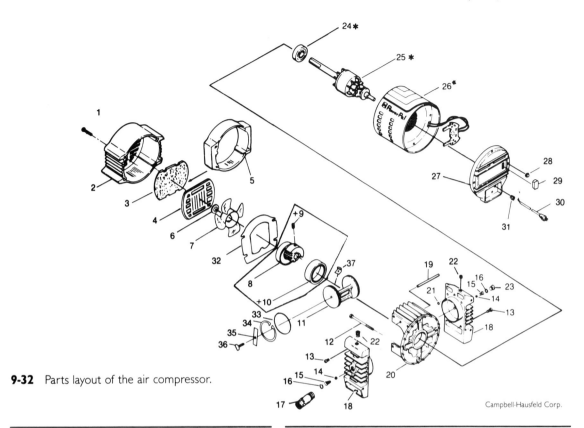

9-32 Parts layout of the air compressor.

Campbell-Hausfeld Corp.

KEY NO.	PART NO.	DESCRIPTION	QTY.
1	ST076403AV	Screw 10-24 x 2-3/4	4
2	MT205900AV	Shroud Assembly Including	1
		MT011300AV Filter and	1
		MT010900AV Retainer	1
3	MT011300AV	Filter	1
4	MT010900AV	Plastic Retainer	1
5	MT011900AV	Fan Shroud Extension	1
6	ST063100AV	Retainer Ring	1
7	MT000900AV	Fan	1
8	MT205200AJ	Eccentric	1
9	+	Set Screw	1
10	+	Ball Bearing	1
11	MT200403AJ	Piston Assembly Including	1
		Key Nos. 34, 35, 36, 37	
12	ST110403AV	Bolt Motor	8
13	ST110102AV	Screw, Phil. Hd.	2
14	MT001800AV	Ball, Check	2
15	MT001900AV	Spring	2
16	ST110700AV	O-Ring	1
17	MT004600AV	Straight Compression Fitting	1
18	MT205600AJ	Head and Cylinder Assembly	1
19	MT001001AP	Tube	1
20	MT350000AJ	End Bell, Front Assembly	1
21	ST110800AV	O-Ring	2
22	ST022400AV	Plug 1/4-18 NPTF	1

KEY NO.	PART NO.	DESCRIPTION	QTY.
23	MT000300AV	Plug	1
24	*	Ball Bearing	1
25	*	Rotor	1
26	*	Stator/Decal Assembly	1
27	MT205100AJ	End Bell, Rear Assembly	1
28	ST074903AV	Acorn Nut	4
29	MT004800AV	Cover Plate for Tank Mtd.	1
		Units	1
30	EC001100AV	Cord and Plug	1
31	ST043500AV	Strain Relief	1
32	MT002100AV	Safety Guard (1 HP)	1
33	MT011700AV	O-Ring Energizer	2
34	MT002500AV	Ring	2
35	LT013400AV	Flapper Value	2
36	ST110101AV	Screw	2
37	MT010700AV	Wear Button	2

+ Available only as part of assembly MT205200AJ
* Available only as part number:
    MT350000AJ   Replacement Unit
Available only as part of assembly:
    MT205100AJ   Rear End Bell Including Key Nos. 28, 30, 31, 32
              and DK154500AV Decal C.H.

Table 9-2. Troubleshooting Chart for Air Compressor

Problem	Causes	Remedy
1. Motor hums or runs slowly when first turned on, but compressor does not start. Motor then stops humming. —Fuses blow —Circuit breakers trip —Motor Thermal Overload Protector trips	1. Light duty extension cord being used. 2. Too many lights or appliances being operated on the same circuit as the compressor (circuit overload). 3. Defective check valve. 4. Low voltage. 5. Incorrect size fuse or circuit breaker 6. Defective motor. 7. Lack of proper ventilation / room temperature.	1. Use additional hose instead of extra extension cord or use heavier gauge extension cord. (See Electrical Information) Check circuit breaker, fuse and thermal overload protector before trying to restart compressor. before trying to restart compressor. before trying to restart compressor. 2. Try another circuit or remove the appliances or lights from circuit being used. 3. Replace or repair. 4. Check with voltmeter. 5. Check for proper fuse. 6. Replace motor. 7. Move compressor to well ventilated area.
2. Compressor will not operate.	1. Power cord not plugged in. 2. On/Off Switch in "Off" position. 3. Motor thermal overload protector tripped. 4. Fuse blown and/or circuit breaker is tripped. 5. Defective motor.	1. Plug power cord in. 2. Switch to "On." 3. Turn On/Off Switch to the "Off" position and wait for unit to cool. Thermal overload protector will automatically reset motor when cooled. After unit has reset turn switch to "On" position. 4. Replace fuse or reset circuit breaker. 5. Replace or repair.
3. Noisy operation	1. Loose pump, motor fasteners, clamps, or accessories. 2. Piston hitting the head. 3. Worn main bearings, broken piston, worn wrist pins, wrist pin bearings, or loose connecting rod bolt.	1. Turn unit off and unplug. Tighten where necessary. 2. Take to Authorized Service Center. 3. Take to Authorized Service Center.

Problem	Possible Cause	Solution
4. Excessive Vibrations.	1. Bent crankshaft.	1. Take to Authorized Service Center.
5. Air blowing from inlet.	1. Broken inlet (reed) valve.	1. Replace valve and gasket.
6. Insufficient pressure at tool or accessory being used.	1. Leaks or restrictions.	1. Check for leaks or restrictions in hose or piping. Repair.
	2. Restricted air intake. (Filter clogged)	2. Clean or replace filter.
	3. Hose or hose connectors too small.	3. Replace with larger hose or connectors.
	4. Air tool requirements are higher than compressor output.	4. Limit the air pressure to the compressor's capacity. Either use a smaller tool or a larger capacity compressor.
	5. Regulator not turned up to high enough pressure.	5. Turn the regulator to proper level.
7. Tank loses pressure rapidly when compressor shuts off.	1. Loose connection (pipe, drain pet-cock, tubing, fitting or hose) or leak.	1. Turn unit off, unplug and tighten.
	2. Faulty check valve.	2. Take to Authorized Service Center.
8. Moisture in discharge air.	1. Condensation or water in tank caused from humidity or compression of air.	1. Drain tank after every use. Drain tank more frequently in humid weather and use an air line filter.
	2. Dirty or clogged filter.	2. Clean or replace filter. See Maintenance.
	3. Improper air ventilation around	3. Keep compressor in well ventilated area.
9. Compressor runs continuously.	1. Air tool requirements higher than compressor output.	1. Limit the air pressure to the compressor's capacity. Either use a smaller tool or a larger capacity compressor.

Wilke Machinery Co.

9-33 A 6-inch table jointer.

For accurate work in most jointing operations, the rear table of the jointer must be exactly level with the knives at their highest point of revolution. This means that the knives must be parallel to the table and project from the cutterhead. Raise or lower the rear table as required by the manufacturer's jointing procedures.

When jointing warped pieces, take light cuts until the surface is flat. Do not force warped material against the table: Excessive pressure will cause the material to spring while passing the knives, and it will remain curved after the cut is completed.

Safety

In addition to following general rules of power tool safety, consider these as well when using the jointer:

- Keep the cutterhead sharp and free of all rust and pitch.
- Always use a push block when jointing stock that does not allow a reasonable distance of safety for your hands.
- Always make sure the exposed cutter head behind the fence is guarded, especially when jointing near the edge.
- Do not perform jointing operations on material shorter than 8 inches, narrower than ¾ inch, or less than ¼ inch thick.
- Maintain the proper relationship of in-feed and out-feed on the table surfaces and in the cutterhead knife path.
- Support the material adequately at all times during operation. Maintain control of the work at all times.
- Do not back the work toward the in-feed table.
- Do not make cuts deeper than ⅛ inch in a single pass. On cuts more than 1½ inches wide, adjust depth cut for 1/16 inch or less. This will avoid overloading the machine and minimize chances of kickback.
- Do not attempt to perform a difficult or little-used operation without studying and figuring out how to use the hold-down and push blades, jigs, fixtures, stops, etc.

Maintenance

Keep the cutterhead free of dirt, dust, and grease to obtain the necessary tight fit. Remove the cutterhead and clean it. Keep the blades sharp: A sharp blade works better and will have a longer life. The blades may be touched up using a whetstone or oilstone. Place the stone over the front table, hold cutterhead down, and slide the stone back and forth across the knife edge—sharpening the knife blade (FIG. 9-34).

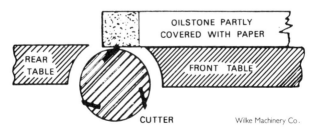

9-34 Sharpening the cutter knives using a whetstone.

To prevent rust on the table and fence of jointer, apply paste wax. Use rust remover if rust has already formed. Use light grease on steel adjusting screws. Occasionally, apply a few drops of light machine oil to the gibs on the right side of each worktable so the base will slide freely. Check all screws and fasteners; keep them tight.

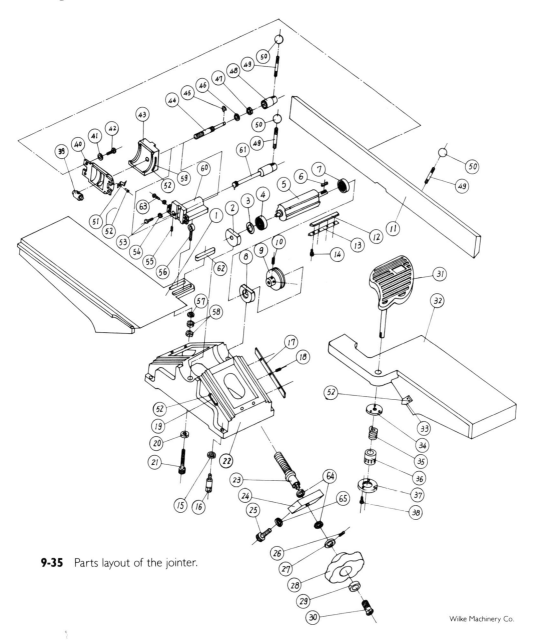

9-35   Parts layout of the jointer.

Wilke Machinery Co.

PARTS LIST

Part No.	Description	Size	Q'ty	Part No.	Description	Size	Q'ty
JC-1	Rear Table		1	JC-34	Retainer Washer		1
JC-2	Bearing Housing	ϕ 35 m/m	1	JC-35	Spring		1
JC-3	Spring Washer	6202 #	1	JC-36	Spring Knob		1
JC-4	Ball Bearing	6202 # ZZ	1	JC-37	Retainer		1
JC-5	Cutter Head Assembly	ϕ 61m/m	1	JC-38	Retainer Screw	5/32"x½"	3
JC-6	Key	5mmx23mm	1	JC-39	Fixing Screw Nut	3/8"-16UNC	1
JC-7	Ball Bearing	6203 # ZZ	1	JC-40	Protractor Scale		1
JC-8	Bearing Housing	ϕ 40m/m	1	JC-41	Washer (flat)	5/16"x ϕ 16	4
JC-9	Pully	2½"	1	JC-42	Hexagon Screw	5/16"x3/4"	4
JC-10	Pully Set Screw	¼"x3/8"	2	JC-43	Protractor Scale		1
JC-11	Fence Body		1	JC-44	Fixed Screw	3/8"	1
JC-12	Knives	6"(152.4m/m)	3	JC-45	E-type Retainer Ring	6mm	1
JC-13	Knife Lock Bar	6"	3	JC-46	Washer (flat)	3/8"	1
JC-14	Hex Screw	¼"x3/8"	12	JC-47	Hexagon nut (Big-type)	3/8"-16UNC	1
JC-15	Spring Washer	3/8"	4	JC-48	Fixing Sleeve		1
JC-16	Nut (Special screw)	3/8"-16 UNC	3	JC-49	Knob Rod	3/8"-16UNC	3
JC-17	Gib	t 3.4m/m	2	JC-50	Knob Head	3/8"-16UNC	3
JC-18	Set Screw	¼"x1"	6	JC-51	Angle Pointer		1
JC-19	Depth Scale		1	JC-52	round heard cross screw	3/16"x3/8"-24 UNC	6
JC-20	Spring Washer	3/8"	2	JC-53	Hexagon Screw	5/16"x1¾"	2
JC-21	Nut	3/8"x1¼"-24UNF	2	JC-54	Nut	5/16"-18UNC	4
JC-22	Base		1	JC-55	Headless Screw	¼"-20UNC	1
JC-23	Adjusting Pole		2	JC-56	Eccentric Shaft Toggle		1
JC-24	Lock Block		2	JC-57	Washer	½"x29	1
JC-25	Lock Screw	5/16"x1¼"	4	JC-58	Screw nut	½"-20UNF	2
JC-26	Roll Pin		1	JC-59	Angle indicator		1
JC-27	Lock Washer		2	JC-60	Slide		1
JC-28	Handle Wheel		2	JC-61	Eccentric Shaft		1
JC-29	Washer	¼"x16mm	2	JC-62	Chain		1
JC-30	Handle Screw	¼"x½"	2	JC-63	Hexagon Screw	5/16"x1"	2
JC-31	Cutter Hand Guard		1	JC-64	Copper washer	3/8"	4
JC-32	Front Table		1	JC-65	Spring washer	5/16"	4
JC-33	Depth Scale		1				

9-35 Continued.

Follow the manufacturer's assembly diagram when you remove a component and do not know how to replace it correctly (FIG. 9-35). Check the motor pulley and belt alignment when the machine seems to be slowing down. Inspect the motor bearings for overheating. Check the motor as you would any other large tool.

LARGE PLANER/MOLDER

The large planer/molder is usually mounted on a separate stand and may contain a saw attachment (FIG. 9-36). On large 3 or 5 horsepower motors, the motor pulleys rotate drive belts to the cutterhead and ripsaw assemblies. These larger motors are operated from a single-phase 230-volt line, pulling from 12 to 25 amps. The 3 horsepower motor may be protected with a 20-amp fuse while the 5 horsepower motor operates on a 30-amp fuse (FIG. 9-37).

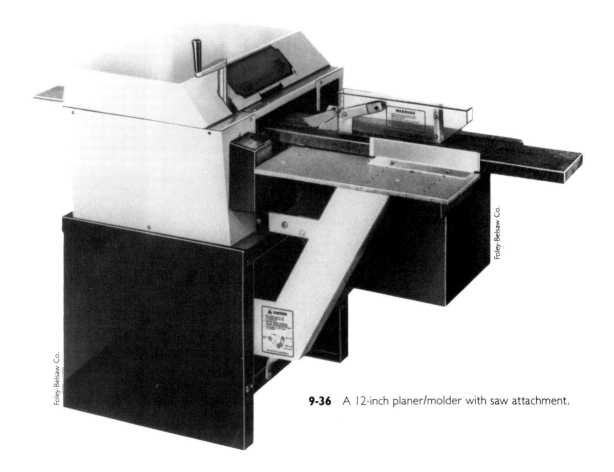

9-36 A 12-inch planer/molder with saw attachment.

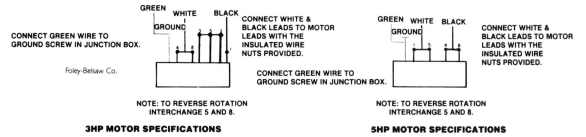

9-37 Motor wiring lead connections on a 3 horsepower motor and a 5 horsepower motor.

General maintenance

There are many different pattern knives that can be used with this machine. Sharpen the knives when the edge shows wear (FIG. 9-38). If the planer knives contain several nicks or burrs on the cutting edge, try to stagger the different knives in the cutting path. Take out the small nicks with a whetstone.

Periodic maintenance

A buildup of sawdust and other debris can cause the machine to plane and mold inaccurately. Periodic cleaning and waxing is recommended. Wipe off close-fitting parts—such as gibs and the planer cutterhead slots—with an oily cloth. Do not soak parts in oil and do not over oil—it defeats the purpose of lubrication and can hasten the collection of dust and shavings. Most bearings on the cutterhead are factory lubricated and sealed. Coat corner screws with grease or rust preventative (FIG. 9-39).

To prevent rust and reduce friction, apply paste wax to the planer bed. Remove resin and other accumulations from feed rolls and bed with a non-flammable solvent. Refer to TABLE 9-3 for a troubleshooting guide to the planer/molder.

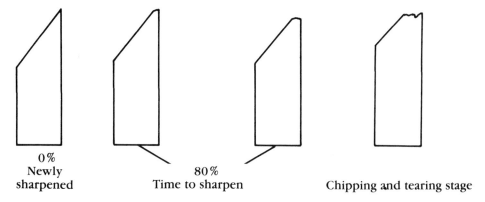

9-38 Sharpen a pattern knife after 80% possible use.

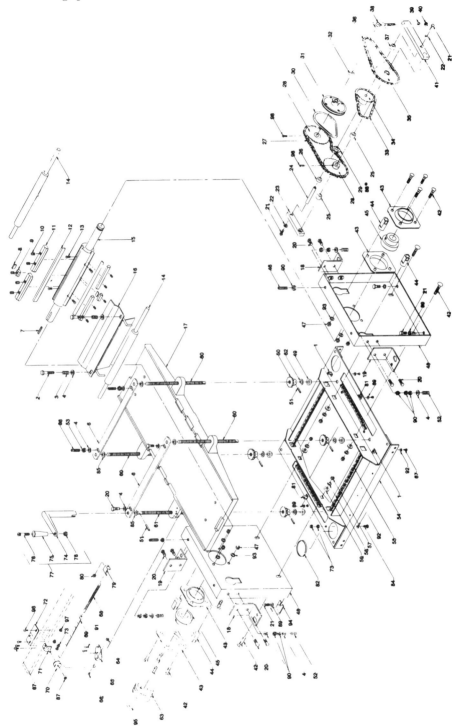

9-39   Exploded view of the 12 inch planer/molder parts list.   Foley-Belsaw Co.

DIAGRAM NUMBER	PART NUMBER	PART DESCRIPTION
45	4509071	Ball Bearing w/Eccentric Lock
46	C374820	Socket Set Screw 3/8-16 NC x 3" Long
47	J502000	Hex Jam Nut 1/2-13 NC
48	4509522	Side Frame
49	4509246	Base Spacer
50	4549033	Corner Sprocket
51	R000872	Roll Pin 1/4" Diameter x 1-1/8" Long
52	4509067	Feed Roll Tension Spring
53	J372000	Hex Jam Nut 3/8-16 NC
54	4509530	Base
55	4509045	#42 Roller Chain
57	J501000	Hex Nut 1/2-13 NC
58	R000473	Lockwasher 1/2 Split
59	R000529	Plain Washer 1/2 SAE
60	4509051	Corner Screw
61	4509081	Corner Crank Screw
62	4509092	Machinery Bushing
63	4509449	Pulley (2) Groove
64	J161000	Hex Nut 8-32 NC
65	4509407	Scale Bracket
66	B160602	Round Head Cap Screw 8-32 NC x 3/8" Long
67	B190609	Phillips Round Head Cap Screw 10-24 NC x 3/8"
68	4509452	Extension Spring
69	4509406	Scale
70	4509421	Scale Roller
71	4509508	Roller Bracket
72	4509378	Scale Window
73	R000553	Kep Nut 10-24 NC
74	4509403	Crank
75	3709457	Handle
76	B313611	Socket Cap Screw 5/16-18 NC x 2-1/4" Long
77	4509503	Crank Handle Assembly
78	J312000	Hex Jam Nut 5/16-18 NC
79	4509454	Spring Clip
80	R000553	Kep Nut 10-24 NC
81	3709417	100° Weldnut
82	4509457	Grommet
84	B191201	Hex Cap Screw 10-24 NC x 3/4" Long
85	3709022	Thrust Washer
86	C372820	Slotted Head Set Screw 3/8-16 NC x 1-3/4"
87	3709142	Push on Retaining Ring
*88	4509583	17-Tooth Sprocket (Optional Equipment)
89	R000481	(2) #1/4 Ext. Star Washer
90	J371000	3/8 Hec Nut
91	B250617	1/4-20 Phillips Rd Hd Cap Screw
92	R000483	Int Tooth
93	R000473	Lockwasher 1/2 Split
94	4509381	Chain Tightner
95	3309059	Decal Rotation
96	B160813	Phillips Round Hd Screw 8-32 NC x 1/2"
97	R000558	Kep Nut 8-32 NC
98	C311007	Square Hd Cap Screw 5/16-18 NC x 5/8"

* - OPTIONAL EQUIPMENT

DIAGRAM NUMBER	PART NUMBER	PART DESCRIPTION
1	3709416	90° Weldnut
2	A375601	Hex Machine Screw 3/8-16 NC x 3-1/2″ Long
3	3709072	Spring
4	R000527	Plain Washer 3/8 SAE
6	4509392	Top Support Bar
7	R000868	Square Key 3/8 Sq. x 1-1/2″ Long
8	4509169	Spacer
9	4509069	Gib 1″
10	C371061	Socket Set Screw 3/8-24 NF x 5/8″ Long
11	4509070	Gib 5-3/4″
12	4501958	Planer Knives
13	B251223	Flat Head Socket Screw 1/4-28 NF x 3/4″ Long
14	4509062	Feed Roll
15	4509054	Cutterhead
16	4509523	Chipbreaker
17	4509400	Bed
18	4509555	Right Bracket
19	4509556	Left Bracket
20	B371201	Hex Cap Screw 3/8-16NC x 3/4″
21	B251001	Hex Cap Screw 1/4-20 NC x 5/8″ Long
22	R000469	Lockwasher
23	4509513	Inner Link Bearing Assembly
24	4509415	Shaft Link
25	4509410	Spacer
26	4509414	Spacer
27	4509418	Roller Chain (91 pitches includes connector)
28	4509034	Sprocket
29	4509527	Small Sprocket Assembly
30	4509027	"V" Belt
31	4509428	Pulley Assembly
32	4509409	Spacer
33	4509420	Roller Chain (48 pitches includes connector)
34	4509525	Sprocket Hub Assembly
35	4509524	Plate Sprocket Assembly
36	4509419	Roller Chain (74 pitches includes connector)
37	4509411	Spacer
38	4509532	Link Adjusting Assembly
39	R000524	Plain Washer 1/4 SAE
40	R000380	Hex Nut Nylok 1/4-20 NC
41	4509529	Outer Link Bearing Assembly
42	E402400	Carriage Bolt 1/2-13 NC x 1-1/2″ Long
43	4509405	Bearing Plate
44	4509417	Bearing Feed Roll

9-39 Continued.

Table 9-3. Troubleshooting Chart for Planer/Molder

Problem	Cause	Remedy
Snipe	1. Dull knives. 2. Inadequate support of long boards. 3. Uneven feed roll pressure front to back. 4. Corner screws loose. 5. Lumber not butted properly.	1. Sharpen knives. 2. Support long boards with extension rollers. 3. Adjust feed roll tension per the instructions. 4. Tighten corner screws per instructions. 5. Butt end to end each place of stock as they pass thru.
Planing Problems		
Fuzzy Grain	Planing wood with a high moisture content.	Remove high moisture content from wood by drying.
Torn Grain	1. Too heavy a cut. 2. Knives cutting against grain. 3. Dull knives.	1. Review proper depth of cut instructions. 2. Review planing for finish. 3. Sharpen knives per instructions.
Rough/Raised Grain	1. Dull knives. 2. Too heavy a cut. 3. Moisture content too high.	1. Sharpen knives per instructions. 2. Review proper depth of cut instructions. 3. Remove high moisture content from wood by drying.
Rounded Glossy Surface	Dull knives.	Sharpen knives per instructions.
Molding Problems		
Wavering Molding Pattern	1. Improper guide set-up. 2. Horizontal play of planer bed table.	1. Review proper guide set-up for molding. 2. Remove play in planer bed per the instructions.
Tear Out at End of Molding	1. Improper guide set-up. 2. Inadequate outfeed pressure.	1. Review proper guide set-up for molding. 2. Adjust feed roll tension per instructions.
Poor Feeding of Lumber	1. Inadequate feed roll pressure. 2. Motor V-belt slipping. 3. Planer bed rough or dirty. 4. Transmission V-belt slipping. 5. Surface of feed rollers too smooth.	1. Adjust feed roll tension per instructions. 2. Tighten or replace motor V-belts per instructions. 3. Clean pitch and residue, and wax planer bed per instructions. 4. Tighten transmission V-belt. 5. Lightly roughen the feed roller surface with a piece of sandpaper.

Table 9-3. Continued.

Uneven Depth of Cut Side to Side	1. Knife projection not uniform. 2. Cutterhead not leveled to planer bed.	1. Adjust knife projection per instructions. 2. Level bed or cutterhead per instructions.
Table Adjust Difficult	1. Corner screw too tight. 2. Lubricate corner screws.	1. Adjust corner screws per the instructions. 2. Lubricate corner screws per the instructions.
Board Thickness Does Not Match Depth of Cut Scale	Depth of cut scale incorrect.	Adjust depth of cut scale per instructions.
Chain Jumping	1. Inadequate tension. 2. Sprockets misaligned. 3. Sprockets worn.	1. Adjust chain tension per instructions. 2. Align sprockets. 3. Replace sprockets.
On/Off Switch Won't Turn On	Locking key missing.	Replace locking key.
Mechanical/Electrical Machine Won't Start/Restart	1. Not plugged in. 2. Hood not in down position. 3. Circuit breaker/fuse. 4. Motor failure. 5. Loose wire. 6. Overload auto reset has not reset. 7. Motor starter failure. 8. Failed or broken interlock switch. 9. Interlock switch not activating. 10. Failed or broken On/Off switch.	1. Check power source. 2. Place hood in down position. 3. Check power source. 4. Have motor checked by qualified electrician per the electrical schematics. 5. Have motor checked by qualified electrician per the electrical schematics. 6. Allow machine to cool down and restart. 7. Have motor starter checked by qualified electrician per the electrical schematics. 8. Have a qualified electrician replace the interlock switch per the electrical schematics. 9. Adjust the interlock switch setting per the instructions. 10. Have a qualified electrician replace the on/off switch per the electrical schematics.
Repeated Circuit Tripping Resulting In Motor Stoppage	Incorrect setting of the amperage overload sensor.	Adjust the amperage overload sensor per the instructions.

Chapter 10

Garage and flea market tools

Power tools picked up at garage sales and flea markets might cost only a few dollars. Sometimes they can be placed back into operation with nothing more than a good cleaning, or a new power cord and brushes. Always, try to purchase these small power tools for under $10 (FIG. 10-1). If the tool costs too much to repair, use it for spare parts.

Inspect the power tool for cracked or broken parts. Is the outside case or body fairly new and clean? Check the power cord for breaks or broken ac plug. Are the body screws stripped or worn? Pass it up if it looks like someone has used a hammer on the case. Does the power tool operate? If possible, peek inside and check for excess oil on the armature or coils. Perhaps a good cleaning is all that is needed in this case.

After purchasing the power tool, take a quick continuity measurement of the ac cord. Connect the low-ohm scale of the meter across the ac plug and turn the ac switch on (FIG. 10-2). No measurement might indicate a short or burned field and armature coils. The average normal resistance measurement of power tools should be between 4 and 22 ohms.

HAND DRILL

This small hand drill was picked up for a dollar at a garage sale (FIG. 10-3). The power tool was fairly clean but the cord was missing. The chuck could be rotated by hand and was not damaged. You can't go wrong spending so little, even if the tool ends up in the parts bin.

I began working on the drill by first removing the screws and taking off the whole body to get at the brushes. The brushes appeared normal but the armature was dirty. A continuity measurement at the cut cord was around 12 ohms, indicating normal field coils.

10-1 Three small power tools picked up at flea markets and garage sales.

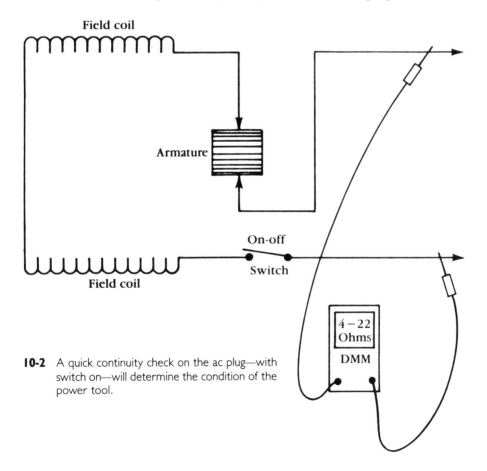

10-2 A quick continuity check on the ac plug—with switch on—will determine the condition of the power tool.

10-3 This small hand drill was picked up for a dollar at a garage sale.

Besides cleaning the armature surface, I washed out and lubricated the bearings. I removed the brushes from their holders, wiped them off, and stretched the springs out to make greater contact (FIG. 10-4). All armature soldered contacts were in good shape. I inspected the connections of the field coils; one connection was barely holding on with two strands of wire. I cleaned and soldered both brush and field coil connections. I then installed a new heavy-duty power cord and soldered all connections (FIG. 10-5). When completed, the power drill continuity was 10.2 ohms. After cleaning the outside metal case with cleaning fluid, I used a buffing wheel and the power tool body looked like new.

SABER SAW

The saber saw had a missing screw in the base plate and one in the body. Probably the power tool had been opened up and one screw was lost (FIG. 10-6). Although the body was intact, the saber saw had been used extensively. Naturally, the blade shaft could not be moved to determine if the unit had frozen bearings. I purchased the saber saw for $1.50.

The saber saw had a continuity measurement of 37 ohms, indicating poor brush contact and connections. I took off the handle assembly by removing two metal screws (FIG. 10-7). I removed the brushes by opening the bottom plate and used a screwdriver to take out each brush. One was worn clear down, but I replaced both. The back brush cover was taken off by removing one screw underneath and one above the end cover (FIG. 10-8).

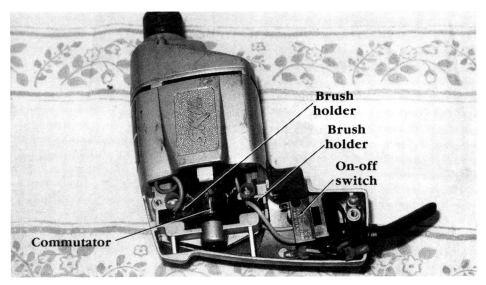

10-4   The brushes were removed, springs stretched, and armature cleaned for better contact.

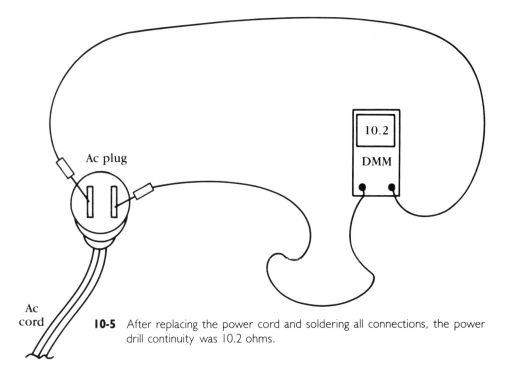

10-5   After replacing the power cord and soldering all connections, the power drill continuity was 10.2 ohms.

10-6   A screw was missing in the base plate and one in the body of the saber saw.

10-7   Remove the screws holding the handle and the screws holding the gear box assembly.

10-8   Removing the end cover of the saber saw to reveal the brushes and commutator.

I removed and cleaned the armature, then brightened it up with sandpaper. I washed out and lubricated the bearings and the shaft assembly. Finally, I cut 2 inches off the ac cord and installed a new plug. After all repairs, the saber saw continuity resistance measured 14.7 ohms.

CIRCULAR SAW

This circular power saw was purchased for $5 (FIG. 10-9). The metal body was quite clean and the on/off switch action appeared normal. The saw blade was fairly new, and that alone made it a bargain.

A continuity resistance measurement at the ac plug proved fatal; there was no measurement. Either the cord, brushes, field coils, armature, or ac switch had to be open. Clicking the switch rapidly off and on still gave no meter indication. I removed the six body and two brush screws, and opened up the body for inspection.

The copper commutator was almost black, indicating that the saw had been stored away without being used for a long time. A continuity check with the ohmmeter from one side of the ac plug to the first brush holder was good. A check of the other brush holder from ac terminal to armature commutator gave no reading.

10-9 This circular saw was purchased for $5. Six body and two brush screws were removed to open up the motor assembly.

I took another measurement, from brush holder to commutator, which indicated an open measurement (FIG. 10-10).

I inspected the motor brush and found the brush was riding high and did not touch the commutator. Either the brush was worn down or it was hung up somewhere. I removed the brush holder assembly, which revealed a cracked outside plastic insulator. The brush would not move out of the holder. After I removed the brush assembly, I found that the metal spring was bent over, preventing pressure to the graphite brush.

I cleaned out the inside of the brass brush holder and applied light oil, then wiped off the excess oil. I stretched out the brush spring before inserting it into the brush holder (FIG. 10-11). Now the brush moved easily out of the holder.

Before replacing both brush holders, I pulled the armature and brightened up the commutator with sandpaper. I washed out both armature end bearings and lubricated them with light oil. The bearings appeared normal, with no side play that might indicate worn bearings. I repaired the plastic brush holder with epoxy cement. After replacing the brushes, the continuity at the ac plug measured 4.7 ohms.

Although the circular saw operated perfectly, I replaced the ac cord because it had a few check marks. I then checked the on/off switch and replaced the power cord with the motor assembly wide open. I replaced the missing body and depth adjustment screws with new screws I had purchased at the hardware store.

With a little elbow grease, replaced brushes, and ac cords, these three power tools were back in action for only a few bucks.

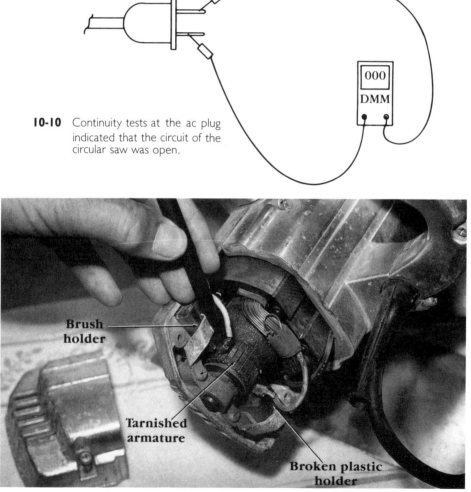

10-10 Continuity tests at the ac plug indicated that the circuit of the circular saw was open.

Brush holder

Tarnished armature

Broken plastic holder

10-11 The brush holder was removed and cleaned out, and the brush spring stretched out and inserted in the repaired plastic holder.

Chapter **11**

Two universal projects

*I*n this chapter are two different universal projects: one that will help keep nickel-cadmium batteries charged, the other a universal speed controller for the ac drill or router. The universal speed controller varies the speed of a universal motor pulling 2.5 amps. The nickel-cadmium battery charger keeps small chargeable batteries ready for action.

UNIVERSAL SPEED CONTROLLER

The universal speed controller will regulate the speed of universal motors found in the 2.5-amp power tool (FIG. 11-1). The circuit is built around a Quadrac, which looks like any regular triac component, but consists of a diac-trigger component mounted in the same package as the triac (FIG. 11-2). The DUT is a bi-directional ac switch and is gate controlled.

The circuit

The controller has a 15-amp fuse, with one side of the load connected to the three-prong ac receptacle. The power tool is plugged into this outlet and the speed is controlled with the variable resister (FIG. 11-3). Only seven components are used in this speed controller.

Although an 8-amp Quadrac component is used here, the 4-amp 400-volt type may be used instead. The component is mounted directly upon a transistor power output heat sink. This heat sink is bolted to several layers of metal, with spacers between to allow a greater amount of heat to radiate. The heat sink must radiate at least 500 watts of power (FIG. 11-4). This 8-amp component may control universal power tools pulling up to 1000 watts with a layer heat sink.

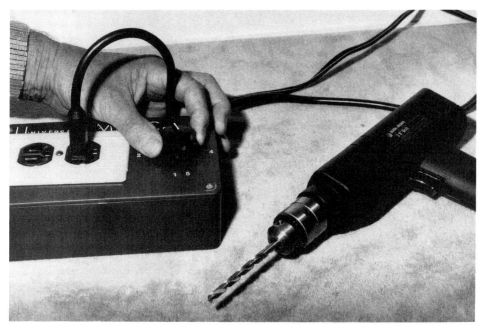

11-1   The completed speed controller operating a 2.5-amp universal power drill.

11-2   The Quadrac component looks like a regular triac component, except the diac and triac components are found in one body.

Wiring the controller

The regular ac outlet and variable speed resistor are mounted on the front cover, while the Quadrac is mounted on the heat sink. All components are soldered up with Number 18 flexible hookup wire. You may use Number 18 single-wire rubber power cord. Referring to FIG. 11-5, the MT1 terminal of the Q 4015 LT part is connected to one side of the ac outlet. MT2 is connected to the other side of the power line and C1. Terminal T connects to one side of variable resistor R2. Make sure the ground wire of ac cord is connected to the ac receptacle green screw.

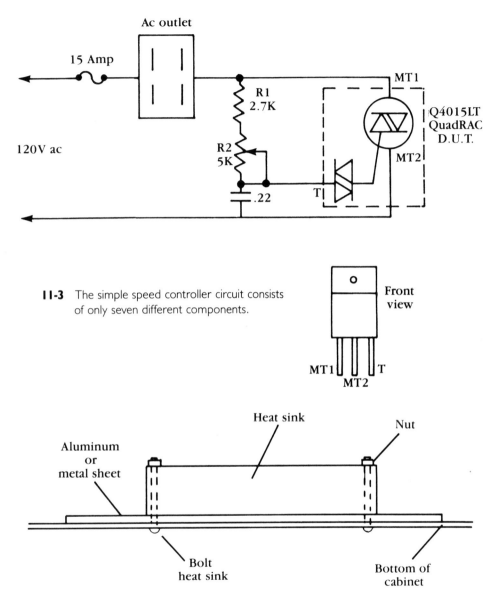

11-3 The simple speed controller circuit consists of only seven different components.

11-4 The controller is mounted upon a regular power transistor heat sink with added metal that is spaced to radiate heat.

Running a check

Plug the power tool into the ac outlet. Set the variable control about halfway. Now plug the voltage controller into the power receptacle. Click on the ac switch of the power tool. Rotate the control slowly upward and then down. Notice how the speed of the power tool is controlled. The power tool might quit at end of rotation, and if the speed is set extremely low, the power tool might not start up properly. In our test, the ac voltage was lowered to 38 volts ac, operating a 2.5 amp drill. After operating the controller for five minutes, check the heat sink for overheating. The power transistor is adequate for 2.5-amp power tools. If 8-amp power tools are used, you might need to add more heat sink.

See TABLE 11-1 for the universal speed controller parts list. To order parts, contact Digi-Key Corp., and Mouser Electronics, listed under "Sources."

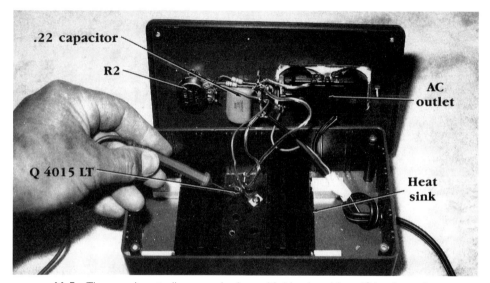

11-5   The speed controller was wired up with Number 16 or 18 hookup wire.

Table 11-1. Parts List for Universal Speed Controller

F1	10-amp fuse socket
C1	.22 capacitor, 400 volts
R1	2.7 K 1-watt resistor
R2	5 K variable linear resistor
DUT	Teccor Quadrac #Q4015 LT (Digi-Key Corp.)
1	Regular three-prong ac outlet and plate
1	Heat sink HS117 Transistor power type (Digi-Key Corp.)
Misc.	Plastic container, heavy-duty ac power cord, solder, nuts and bolts

UNIVERSAL NICKEL-CADMIUM BATTERY CHARGER

Most nickel-cadmium battery chargers consist of a step-down power transformer, rectifier, cord, and male plug. This universal battery charger consists of the same elements, except the power transformer has several voltage taps (FIG. 11-6). T1 steps the ac voltage down to 3, 4.5, 6, 9, and 12 volts. This battery charger will charge up many different combinations of nickel-cadmium batteries.

11-6   The universal nickel-cadmium battery charger may be used to charge batteries from 1.2 to 12 volts dc.

Schematic diagram

Like all nickel-cadmium cordless power tool battery chargers, this one is simple in design and has various dc voltage outputs. Two rotary switches change the ac and dc output voltages (FIG. 11-7). A 1-amp silicon diode rectifies the halfwave voltage and is applied to the output cables. Because different battery cords are needed for the various power tools, SW2 switches the various cables and plugs.

SW2 is a four-position switch. The off position is at 0. Position 1 is 3 volts, 2 is 4.5 volts, 3 is 6 volts, 4 is 9 volts, and 5 is 12 volts. The various cables are switched into the output with SW2. One of the output cables consists of a pair of color-coded alligator clips that can be clipped to any battery or set of batteries in series. The alligator clips are ideal to charge up portable radio batteries. The red clip runs to the positive battery terminal, the black alligator clip to the negative terminal.

Operation

First, select the correct output cable and plug it into the cordless power tool that is to be charged. Set SW2 to that exact cable output. Make sure the positive terminal from the switch runs to the inside terminal of the male plug. If the small power tool is operated from a 2.9-volt battery source, switch SW1 to the number 2 (4.5-volt) position. If the power tool is operated from a 6-volt dc battery source, switch to the number 4 (9-volt) position (FIG. 11-8). Now plug the charger into the ac receptacle.

Remember, the charging voltage should always be higher than the operating voltage of the power tool. Charge the power tool 1 to 5 hours (refer to the instruction manual). After the new cordless tool has been charged up once, the time required for charging might drop (TABLE 11-2). Charge the nickel-cadmium batteries when the power tool begins to run slowly.

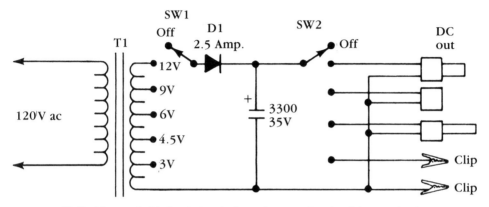

11-7 Like most nickel-cadmium battery chargers, the circuit is very simple.

11-8 Select the correct ac voltage with SW1 and the correct output charging cord with SW2.

Table 11-2. Required AC Voltage vs. DC Voltage

SW1 AC Voltage		DC Battery Voltage
1.	3 V ac	1.5–2.5 V ac
2.	4.5 V ac	2.5–3.6 V dc
3.	6 V ac	3.6 V dc
4.	9 V ac	4.8–7.2 V dc
5.	12 V ac	7.2–12 V dc

Construction

Prepare the front cover by drilling two holes for SW1 and SW2. Drill four holes for the different test cables. In one end, drill a hole for the ac cord. Drill the power transformer holes close to SW1. Mount the transformer on the bottom.

Tie a knot inside the box, leaving about 4 inches of ac cord. This will prevent the ac cord from being yanked out. Solder each color wire of the transformer to the correct switch terminal (FIG. 11-9). Insert the silicon diode between SW1 and SW2. Solder each negative cable wire to the common ground wire. Run the positive lead to the correct terminal on SW2.

11-9 Most nickel-cadmium batteries are charged up after 1 to 3 hours. Follow the manufacturer's instructions.

See TABLE 11-3 for the universal battery charger parts list. To order parts, contact Circuit Specialists, listed under "Sources."

Table 11-3. Parts List for Universal Nickel-Cadmium Battery Charger

T1	Multi-tap step-down ac transformer, 3 V, 4.5 V, 6 V, 9 V and 12 V #41FW300 300 MA (Circuit Specialists)
D1	2.5-amp silicon diode
C1	3300 35-volt electrolytic capacitor
SW1	Six-position SPST rotary switch
SW2	Five-position SPST rotary switch
Cabinet	Plastic or metal box $6 \times 3^{3}/_{16} \times 1^{7}/_{8}$
Misc.	Hookup wire, plugs, ac cord, vinyl grommet

Sources

AEC Power Tool Corp.
Three Shaw's Cove
New London, CT 06320

American Machine & Tool (AMT)
4th Avenue and Spring
Royersford, PA 19468

Arnall Woodworking Machines
161 Avenue of the Americas
New York, NY 10013

Arrow Fastner Co., Inc.
271 Mayhill St.
Saddle Brook, NJ 07662

Black & Decker
10 North Park Ave.
P.O. Box 798
Hunt Valley, MD 21030

Bosch Power Tool Corp.
3701 Neuse Boulevard
New Bern, NC 28560-9399

Bostik Consumer Division
USM Corporation
4408 Pottsville Pike
Reading, PA 19605

Circuit Specialists
P.O. Box 3047
Scottsdale, AZ 85271-3047

Colonial Saw Lamello
100 Pembroke St.
P.O. Box "A"
Kingston, MA 02364

Conover Woodcraft, Inc.
18125 Madison Road
Parkman, OH 44080

Delta International Corp.
246 Alpha Drive
Pittsburgh, PA 15238

Digi-Key Corp.
701 Brooks Ave., South
P.O. Box 677
Thief River Falls, MN 56701-0677

Elektra Beckum USA Corp.
401 Kennedy Blvd., P.O. Box 24
Somerdale, NJ 08083

Elu Tools (Black & Decker)
10 North Park Drive, P.O. Box 798
Hunt Valley, MD 21030

Emco-Marer Corp.
2050 Farrwood Ave.
Columbus, OH 43207

Excalibur Machine & Tool Co.
210 Eight Street South
Lewiston, NY 14092

Foley-Belsaw
6301 Equitable Road, Dept. 91400
Kansas City, MO 64120

Frend USA Inc.
P.O. Box 7187
High Point, NC 27264

General Mfg. Co.
102 Kimball Ave.
So. Burlington, VT

Gilliom Mfg. Co.
Dept. WB-JF9
P.O. Box 1018
St. Charles, MO 63302

Grissly Imports
P.O. Box 2069
Billingham, WA 98227

Harrison Lathes
3400 Covington Road
Kalamazoo, MI 49002

Hegner Scroll Saws
P.O. Box 312
New Castle, DE 19720

Hitachi
4487 - F
Norcross, GA 30093

Houseworks
126 Monroe Turnpike
Trumbull, CT 06611-1316

INCA
161 Avenue of Americas
New York, NY 10013

Jet Equipment & Tools
P.O. Box 1477, 1901 Jefferson Ave.
Tacoma, WA 98402

KITY
Ferris Machinery
309 N. 10th
Blue Springs, MO 64015

Konig-Dreschelbank Lathes
161 Avenue of Americas
New York, NY 10013

Kress Tools of America
126 Monroe Turnpike
Trumbull, CT 06611

Lobo Power Tools
10922 Klingerman St.
S. El Monte, CA 91733

Makita
12950 E. Alandra Blvd.
Cerritos, CA 90701

Metabo Corp.
1231 Wilson Drive
Westchester, PA 19380

Milwaukee Electric Tool Corp.
13135 W. Lisbon Rd.
Brookfield, WI 53005

Mini-Max
5933 A Peachtree Industrial Blvd.
Norcross, GA 30092

Mouser Electronics
P.O. Box 699
Mansfield, TX 76063

Myford Woodcraft
41 Atlantic Ave., P.O. Box 4000
Woburn, MA 01888

Porter Cable
Hwy. 45 at Youngs Crossing
Jackson, TN 38305

Powermatic-Powerstar
McMinnville, TN 37110

Pro Cut
Lancaster Machinery Corp.
715 Fountain Ave.
Lancaster, PA 17601

RBI Industries, Inc.
P.O. Box 369
Harrisonville, MO 64701

Ross Industries, Inc.
P.O. Box 637
Pineville, MO 64856

Ryobi America Corp.
1158 Tower Lane
Nensonville, IL 60106

Sakura USA
360 S. Monroe St.
Xenia, OH 45385

Scheppach Tools
15935 NW 57th Ave.
Hialeah, FL 33014

Sears, Roebuck & Co.
Sears Tower
Chicago, IL 60684

Shopsmith
3931 Image Drive
Dayton, OH 45414

Skil Corporation
4801 West Peterson
Chicago, IL 60646

The Stanley Works
Stanley Tools Division
New Britain, CT 06050

Strong Tool Works
20425 Beatrice
Livonia, MI 48152

Super Scroll
American Machinery Sales, Inc.
P.O. Box 5285
Marshalton, DE 19809

Swingline Co.
Division of Swingline, Inc.
32-00 Skillman Ave.
Long Island, NY 11101

Synitech
15935 NW 57th Ave.
Hialeah, FL 33014

The Tool Co.
5271 Raintree Parkway
Lees Summit, MO 64082

Total Shop
P.O. Box 16297
Greenville, SC 29606

Williams & Hussey Machine
RR 101 West
Milford, NH 03055

Woodmaster Tools
2849 Terrace
Dept. "D"
Kansas City, MO 64108

Value Craft Power Tools
3 Craftsman Road
East Windsor, CT 06088

Glossary

ac   Alternating current. The power source supplied by power companies to receptacles in residences. Voltage flows first in one direction, then reverses and flows in the opposite direction, changing several times each second.

amp   Ampere. The unit for measuring the electricity flowing through a motor or power tool.

arbor   A revolving shaft that fits into the drill and holds cutting or grinding tools.

armature   The chuck is connected to the gear box which turns the gears by the motor armature. The motor armature directly drives the motor pulley. A special type of rotor.

battery   A device that provides dc power with chemical reaction to operate the dc motor. Batteries may be wired in series to increase the needed voltage to operate cordless tools.

bearing   A sleeve or ball bearing allows the shaft of the armature or gears to rotate without much friction. Bearings might require lubrication of light oil.

bimetal   Two different metals in one unit that will bend with temperature to control heating and cooling devices. Some glue guns have a bimetal thermostat.

brush   A conductive graphite or carbon material that rides on the armature of the motor as it rotates.

capacitor   The electronic component that stores energy or a charge. Capacitors are used in start-up windings of large motors.

centrifugal switch   The switch that opens the starting capacitor or winding when the armature reaches a certain speed, allowing the motor to run on its own power.

chuck   A device that clamps around a bit on a drill.

circuit   A complete path of electricity flowing from power receptacle through the cord, motor switch, windings, armature, and brushes of a motor or power tool.

circuit breaker   The circuit breaker opens when too much current is drawn through it. The home or shop should have a circuit breaker. When a circuit is overloaded, this electrical device will trip and protect the machinery. The breaker then simply needs to be reset.

clutch   A clutch adjustment is found on larger power tools so you can adjust them to slip at a given torque.

collet   A chuck type device that squeezes down on and holds bits in place.

compressor   A device to control air to run tools, or sand blasting and painting equipment.

commutator   The part of the armature that rotates in the motor. The carbon or graphite brushes lay against the armature as it rotates.

conduit   Metal or plastic tubing through which power wires are run.

cps   Cycles per second.

dc   Direct current. Batteries provide dc voltage to the cordless power tools. The current moves in one direction only.

diode   A rectifying device. Silicon diodes are used in dc battery charging circuits.

DPDT   Double pole, double throw switch. Most are sliding switches used in power tools. The fuse box may contain a DPDT switch connecting and disconnecting two different circuits.

efficiency   The ratio of input power watts compared to the output watts.

electric motor   A device that converts electrical energy to mechanical energy.

electromagnet   A magnet formed from a coil wound around a metal core. A magnetic field develops when current passes through the coil.

field winding   A coil of wire that is wrapped around the motor and that lays next to the metal exterior of the motor. The field coils generate a magnetic field when current is applied.

frequency   The number of complete cycles of ac current per second.

fuse   A safety device that opens when too much current is drawn through a circuit. Fuses are rated in amps. A fuse will withstand the amperage for which it is rated, but will blow or burn out if overloaded—subjected to excessive current.

gauge   A measurement of wire thickness. The lower the gauge number, the larger the wire.

ground   A series of electrical conductors that connect all conductive metal parts of a tool to the earth. The wire that grounds the motor or returns the path of the circuit to ground is usually white. The ground wire in the ac power tool three-prong cord is usually green.

horsepower   A unit of electrical power that equals 746 watts. Motors are rated in horsepower.

hot wire   The black or red positive wire in the electrical power receptacle. The hot wire is always above ground. The hot wire is dangerous: use caution.

IC (integrated circuit)—These are found in power tool voltage regulation circuits.
induced current   The electric current produced by a moving conductor in the magnetic field.
insulation   The protective cover over wire cable.

live circuit   A circuit that carries electrical current.
load   On the power line or batteries of power tools, the tool is the load, which is taking the energy.

microswitch   A small switch with sensitive action.

open circuit   A break in the circuit. A switch in the open, or off position, prevents electricity from flowing.
overload   Operation of electrical equipment in excess of its capacity. Overloading can result in blown fuses, overheating, and damage. The average household fuse is 15 or 20 amps.
overload protector   A device that protects the motor when it becomes overloaded or overheated.

polarized   The ac power tool is polarized with a three-prong plug so it may only be inserted into the receptacle in one direction, maintaining the correct grounding. One side of the ac receptacle is positive (black), the other terminal negative (white) with a metal ground wire that is green. The bronze screw on the ac receptacle is positive.
power factor   The portion of the current delivered to the motor that is used to do work.

relay   A device with a solenoid that switches a circuit. When the solenoid is energized by a voltage, the switch contacts may be closed or opened.
resistance   A force that works against the flow of electrical current. A resistor is measured in ohms.
rheostat   An electronic device with a variable resistance.
romex   A plastic or rubber coated cable to carry electricity to power outlets.
rpm   Revolutions per minute. The speed at which the motor shaft of a power tool revolves.
rotor   The rotating section within the stator of a motor. The rotor consists of core material, windings, commutator, and shaft.

schematic   A drawing of electrical or electronic circuits.
service entrance   The point at which the cable from the power line that provides ac voltage to the fuse box or circuit breaker is connected.
short circuit   An improper connection between two circuit-carrying wires. Usually, fire or sparks result from a short circuit in the ac power lines; this can cause damage to the motor windings.
solder   A mixture of tin and lead that will melt at a low temperature to bond wire connections. The soldering iron is the tool that heats the solder.

solenoid   A coil that surrounds a movable rod. Current moving through the coil causes the rod to move. A solenoid is used to activate various tools.

SPST   Single pole, single throw switch. A SPST switch is used to turn power tool motors on and off.

solderless connectors   Twist or crimp caps that connect electrical connections, making soldered connections unnecessary.

stator   The stationary section of the motor. Consists of outer frame, core, and field windings.

synchronous speed   The constant speed of the motor, depending on the frequency of the power supply and number of poles in the motor.

thermostat   A device sensitive to temperature changes. The thermostat may control the heat of a soldering iron or glue gun.

torque   The measure of rotating force around an axis.

transformer   A device to transform ac energy. The transformer is found in the nickel-cadmium battery chargers of cordless power tools.

voltage   The force that moves electrical energy through a circuit.

VOM   Volt-ohm milliammeter. Measures resistance (ohms), voltage (ac or dc), and current (amps and milliampere).

watt   The unit of electrical power. One watt is dissipated by a resistance of 1 ohm through which a current of 1 ampere flows. Watt is the product of volts and amperes (volts × amperes = watts).

winding   The conductive coils in a motor. These coils may be wrapped or have enameled wire in the field and armature windings.

Index